MathFlare

Name: _______________________

Class: ___________

Teacher: _______________________

Introduction

As parents and educators, we recognize the pivotal role mathematics plays in shaping a child's academic journey and future success. Yet, the path to mathematical proficiency can often seem daunting, fraught with challenges and complexities. That's where the transformative power of MathFlare Workbooks shine through, illuminating the way forward with clarity, precision, and purpose.

Introducing MathFlare Workbooks – a beacon of guidance, a testament to excellence, and a catalyst for achievement. Crafted with meticulous care and expertise, MathFlare Workbooks stand as paragons of educational excellence, designed to nurture young minds, ignite a passion for learning, and develop a deep-rooted understanding of mathematical concepts.

Picture this: your child eagerly delves into the pages of Mathflare Workbook, greeted by a step-by-step guide illuminated with vivid examples that demystify complex mathematical concepts. With each turn of the page, they embark on a journey of discovery, encountering thoughtfully curated practice questions that reinforce learning and hone problem-solving skills. And when they unveil the answers to those very questions, a sense of accomplishment blossoms within them – a tangible reward for their hard work and dedication.

But MathFlare Workbooks are more than just tools for learning; they are pathways to comprehension, fostering a deep-seated understanding of mathematical concepts through a sequential, logical flow. From fundamental principles to advanced problem-solving strategies, every chapter builds upon the last, ensuring a robust foundation upon which future knowledge can be constructed.

As parents, we yearn for nothing more than to see our children thrive, to witness the spark of inspiration ignited within them as they conquer academic challenges with confidence and poise. MathFlare Workbooks serve as partners in this noble endeavor, offering not just practice questions, but the keys to unlocking a world of opportunity.

And for teachers, MathFlare Workbooks stand as invaluable allies in the quest to cultivate mathematical proficiency in the classroom. With answers readily available, instructors can focus on guiding and nurturing their students, confident in the knowledge that MathFlare Workbooks provide a solid framework upon which to build.

In the pages of MathFlare Workbooks, we find not just the promise of academic excellence, but the seeds of a brighter tomorrow. So let us embrace the power of mathematics, let us champion the journey of learning, and let us pave the way for a generation of young minds poised to shape the world. With MathFlare Workbooks as our guide, the possibilities are infinite, and the future, bright.

Table of Contents

MathFlare
Grade 2
MATH WORKBOOK
Step by Step Guide and Essential Practice with Answers
Addition Subtraction
Multiplication
Place Value and Expanded Notations
Geometry
MathFlare Publishing

MathFlare
Grade 2-3
MATH WORKBOOK
Step by Step Guide and Essential Practice with Answers
Addition Subtraction
Multiplication and Division
Place Value and Expanded Notations
Geometry
MathFlare Publishing

MathFlare
Grade 3
MATH WORKBOOK
Step by Step Guide and Essential Practice with Answers
Multiplication and Division
Decimals
Place Value and Expanded Notations
Fractions and Geometry
MathFlare Publishing

MathFlare
Grade 1
MATH WORKBOOK
Step by Step Guide and Essential Practice with Answers
Counting and Numbers
Addition and Subtraction
Place Value and Expanded Notations
Understanding Time
MathFlare Publishing

MathFlare
Grade 1-2
MATH WORKBOOK
Step by Step Guide and Essential Practice with Answers
Counting and Numbers
Addition and Subtraction
Place Value and Expanded Notations
Understanding Time
MathFlare Publishing

MathFlare
Grade 3-4
MATH WORKBOOK
Step by Step Guide and Essential Practice with Answers
Addition Subtraction
Multiplication Division
Place Value and Expanded Notations
Fractions and Geometry
MathFlare Publishing

MathFlare
Grade 4
MATH WORKBOOK
Step by Step Guide and Essential Practice with Answers
Addition Subtraction
Multiplication Division
Place Value and Expanded Notations
Fractions and Geometry
MathFlare Publishing

MathFlare
Grade 4-5
MATH WORKBOOK
Step by Step Guide and Essential Practice with Answers
Multiplication Division
Place Value and Expanded Notations
Fractions and Geometry
Unit Conversion
MathFlare Publishing

MathFlare
Grade 5
MATH WORKBOOK
Step by Step Guide and Essential Practice with Answers
Multiplication Division
Place Value and Expanded Notations
Fractions and Geometry
Unit Conversion
MathFlare Publishing

MathFlare
Grade 5-6
MATH WORKBOOK
Step by Step Guide and Essential Practice with Answers
Multiplication Division
Place Value and Expanded Notations
Fractions and Geometry
Units and Statistics
MathFlare Publishing

MathFlare
Grade 6
MATH WORKBOOK
Step by Step Guide and Essential Practice with Answers
Integers and Statistics
Arithmetic and Pre-Algebra
Fractions and Geometry
Ratio and Percentage
MathFlare Publishing

MathFlare
Grade 6-7
MATH WORKBOOK
Step by Step Guide and Essential Practice with Answers
Arithmetic and Pre-Algebra
Ratio, Percent Proportion
Geometry
Statistics
MathFlare Publishing

MathFlare
Grade 7
MATH WORKBOOK
Step by Step Guide and Essential Practice with Answers
Pre-Algebra
Ratio, Percent Proportion
Geometry
Statistics
MathFlare Publishing

MathFlare
Grade 7-8
MATH WORKBOOK
Step by Step Guide and Essential Practice with Answers
Pre-Algebra
Ratio, Percent Proportion
Geometry and Cartesian Plane
Statistics
MathFlare Publishing

MathFlare
Grade 8-9
MATH WORKBOOK
Step by Step Guide and Essential Practice with Answers
Pre-Algebra
Ratio, Proportion and Percentage
Linear Equations
Geometry and Cartesian Plane
MathFlare Publishing

MathFlare
Grade 8
MATH WORKBOOK
Step by Step Guide and Essential Practice with Answers
Pre-Algebra
Percentage
Linear Equations
Geometry
MathFlare Publishing

Place Value and Expanded Notation

Place value tells us the value of a digit in a number based on where it's placed.

Imagine we have the number 45,643. It has five digits: 4, 5, 6, 4, and 3.

Now, each digit holds a special place. Let's break down the number 45,643:

- The first digit, 4, is in the ten thousands place.

- The second digit, 5, is in the thousands place.

- The third digit, 6, is in the hundreds place.

- The fourth digit, 4, is in the tens place.

- The fifth digit, 3, is in the ones place.

When we add these values together, we find the value of the entire number:

$$40000 + 5000 + 600 + 40 + 3 = 45,643$$

Expanded notation helps us see the individual value of each digit in a number and how they contribute to the overall value of the number. It's like breaking down a big puzzle into smaller pieces to understand it better!

So, in expanded notation, we can write 45,643 as: 40000 (from ten thousand place) + 5000 (from thousands place) + 600 (from the hundreds place) + 40 (from the tens place) + 3 (from the ones place).

Let's solve problems from exercises:

Place value of the underline digit:

$$85,\underline{6}44 = \underline{\text{5 thousands}}$$

Expanded notations:

$\underline{63,698}$ 6 ten thousands + 3 thousands + 6 hundreds + 9 tens + 8 ones

15,643   1 ten thousand + 5 thousands + 6 hundreds + 4 tens + 3 ones

$\underline{64,612}$ 60,000 + 4,000 + 600 + 10 + 2

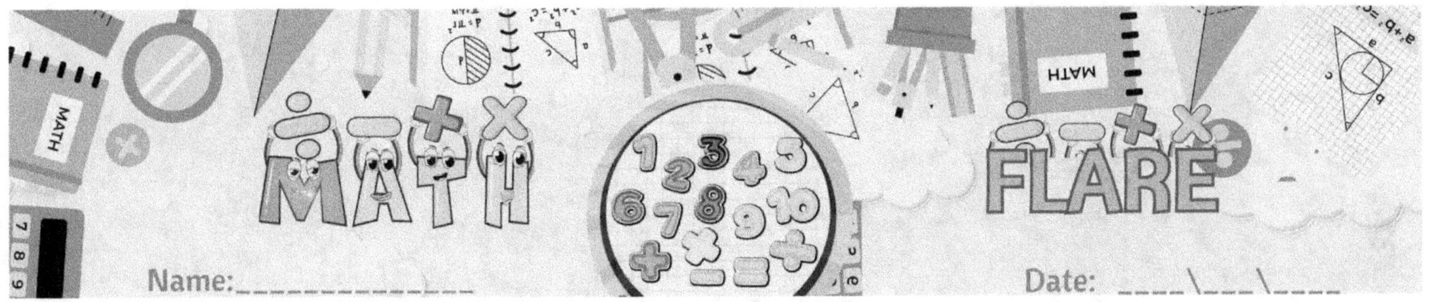

Place Value

Determine the place value of the underlined digit.

1. 1,09<u>6</u> = _______________

2. 9,<u>3</u>34 = _______________

3. <u>1</u>,269 = _______________

4. <u>2</u>,591 = _______________

5. 1,<u>8</u>17 = _______________

6. <u>1</u>,047 = _______________

7. <u>7</u>,944 = _______________

8. 3,3<u>8</u>9 = _______________

9. 3,9<u>5</u>9 = _______________

10. 7<u>6</u>3 = _______________

11. 3,0<u>5</u>4 = _______________

12. 1,48<u>5</u> = _______________

13. 2,<u>0</u>07 = _______________

14. 9,9<u>4</u>0 = _______________

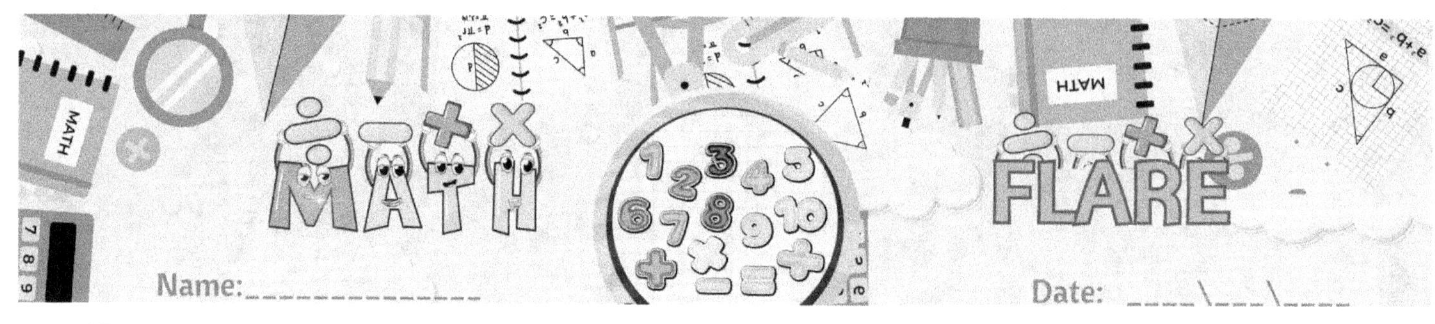

15. 3,882 = _______________________

16. 1,386 = _______________________

17. 4,277 = _______________________

18. 5,975 = _______________________

19. 1,755 = _______________________

20. 7,345 = _______________________

21. 2,539 = _______________________

22. 4,423 = _______________________

23. 2,743 = _______________________

24. 8,010 = _______________________

25. 2,712 = _______________________

26. 1,573 = _______________________

27. 2,342 = _______________________

28. 890 = _______________________

29. 1,474 = _______________________

30. 2,546 = _______________________

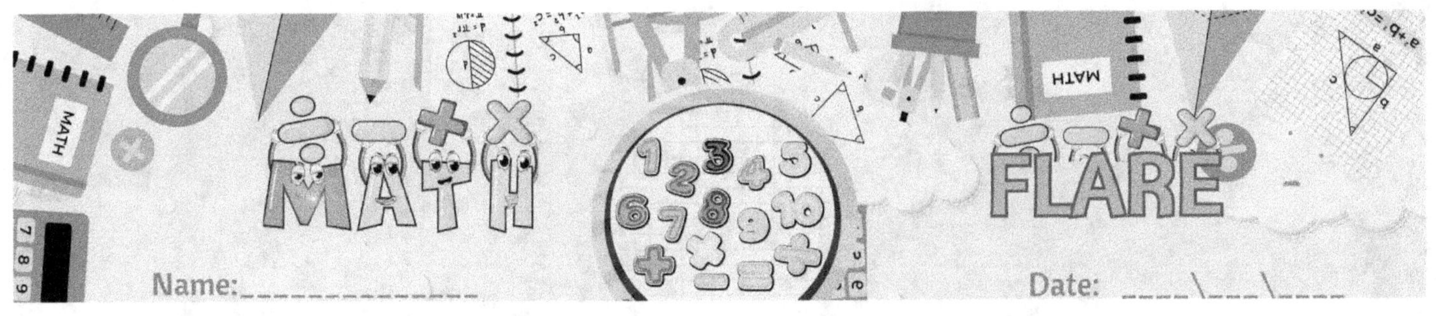

31. 1,9̲04 = _______________

32. 8,74̲9 = _______________

33. 4,2̲61 = _______________

34. 9,8̲47 = _______________

35. 9,63̲4 = _______________

36. 6,79̲8 = _______________

37. 5,07̲7 = _______________

38. 7̲,997 = _______________

39. 5,7̲20 = _______________

40. 2,55̲8 = _______________

41. 8,8̲04 = _______________

42. 2,305̲ = _______________

43. 4,12̲7 = _______________

44. 4,6̲10 = _______________

45. 6̲,012 = _______________

46. 7,79̲0 = _______________

Name:________________   Date: ____________

47. 8,7_6_4 = ______________________

48. _3_,742 = ______________________

49. _4_,292 = ______________________

50. 9,90_8_ = ______________________

51. _2_,354 = ______________________

52. _9_,788 = ______________________

53. _3_,451 = ______________________

54. 5,00_0_ = ______________________

55. 1,8_2_4 = ______________________

56. _6_,672 = ______________________

57. 6,59_2_ = ______________________

58. 3,2_5_8 = ______________________

59. 9,_8_78 = ______________________

60. 24_5_ = ______________________

61. 8,70_4_ = ______________________

62. _7_,054 = ______________________

63. 1,91<u>6</u> = _______________________

64. 1,4<u>1</u>3 = _______________________

65. <u>8</u>,858 = _______________________

66. <u>4</u>,304 = _______________________

67. <u>7</u>,223 = _______________________

68. 2,<u>1</u>59 = _______________________

69. <u>3</u>07 = _______________________

70. 7,0<u>8</u>3 = _______________________

71. 6,<u>3</u>08 = _______________________

72. 6,2<u>7</u>8 = _______________________

73. 2<u>5</u>6 = _______________________

74. 9,1<u>9</u>6 = _______________________

75. <u>8</u>,540 = _______________________

76. 2<u>3</u>5 = _______________________

77. 2<u>9</u>7 = _______________________

78. 8,<u>1</u>32 = _______________________

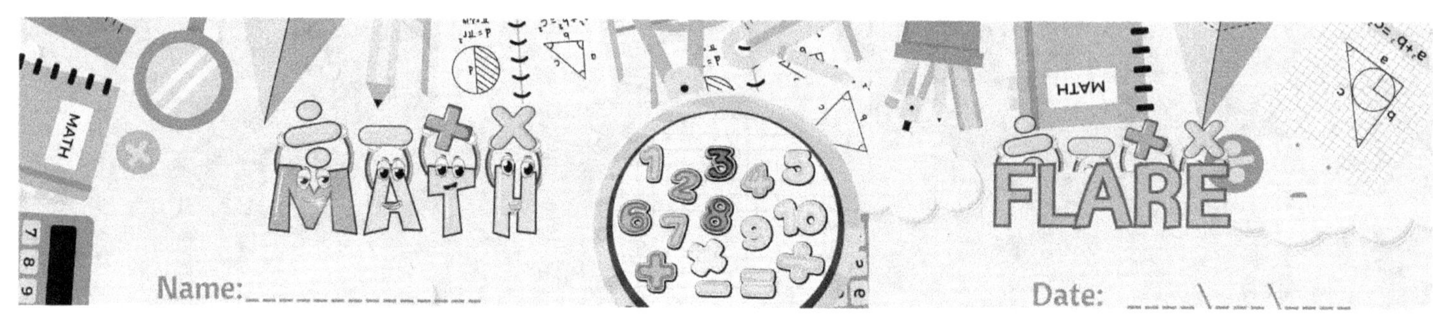

79. 1,9<u>9</u>9 = ___________________

80. <u>4</u>,922 = ___________________

81. 2,<u>8</u>08 = ___________________

82. 8,59<u>9</u> = ___________________

83. 6,5<u>9</u>8 = ___________________

84. 1,5<u>6</u>5 = ___________________

85. <u>1</u>94 = ___________________

86. 2,11<u>4</u> = ___________________

87. 5,29<u>9</u> = ___________________

88. 9,26<u>0</u> = ___________________

89. 8,0<u>2</u>4 = ___________________

90. 2,9<u>6</u>3 = ___________________

91. <u>2</u>07 = ___________________

92. 1,<u>8</u>20 = ___________________

MathFlare - Place Value 2nd and 3rd Grade

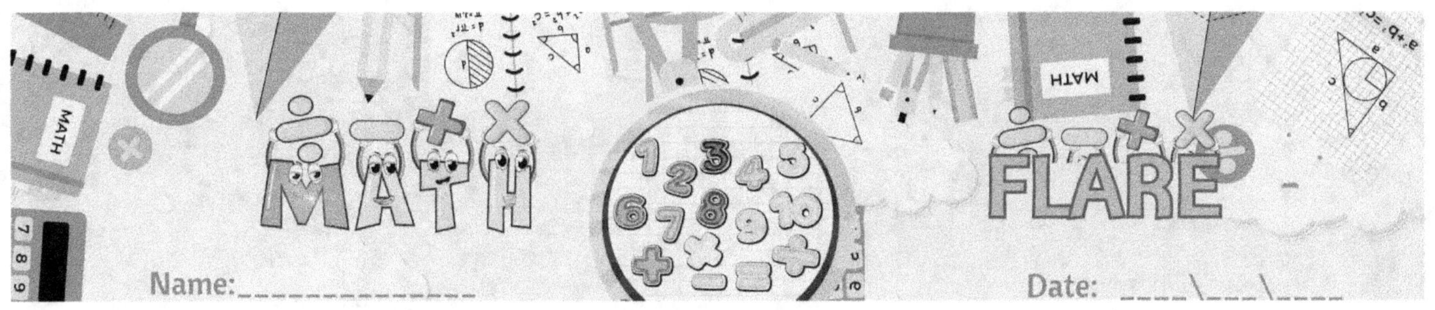

Place Value: Expanded Notation

Provide the expanded notation for each value.

93. _______________ 9 thousands + 4 hundreds + 4 tens + 3 ones

94. _______________ 9 thousands + 6 hundreds + 7 ones

95. _______________ 4 thousands + 8 hundreds + 1 ten + 2 ones

96. _______________ 3 thousands + 9 hundreds + 1 ten + 4 ones

97. _______________ 7 thousands + 6 hundreds + 3 tens

98. _______________ 6 hundreds + 7 tens + 1 one

99. _______________ 6 thousands + 4 hundreds + 7 tens + 7 ones

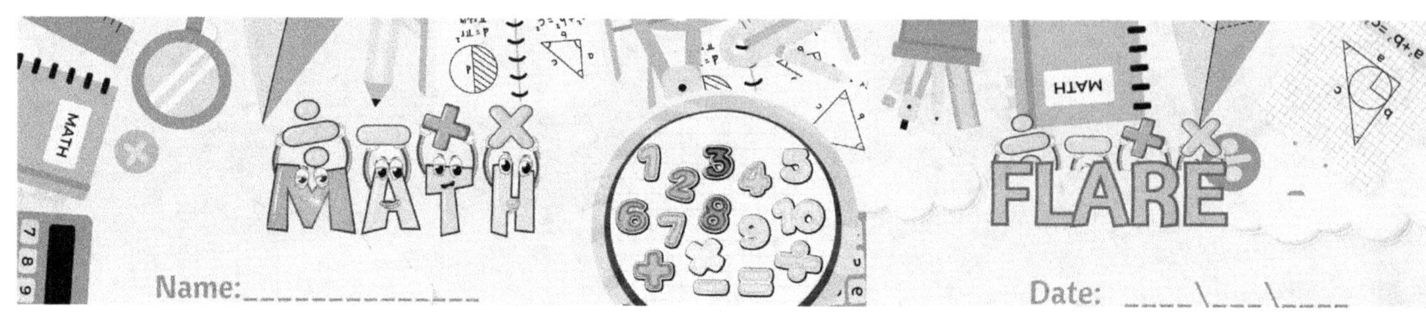

100. _________________ 7 thousands + 6 hundreds + 7 tens + 7 ones

101. _________________ 9 thousands + 2 hundreds + 5 tens + 2 ones

102. _________________ 2 thousands + 9 hundreds + 9 tens + 9 ones

103. _________________ 4 hundreds + 7 tens + 4 ones

104. _________________ 2 thousands + 5 hundreds + 8 tens + 4 ones

105. _________________ 5 hundreds + 6 tens + 3 ones

106. _________________ 8 thousands + 8 hundreds + 9 tens + 8 ones

107. _________________ 7 thousands + 8 hundreds + 1 ten + 4 ones

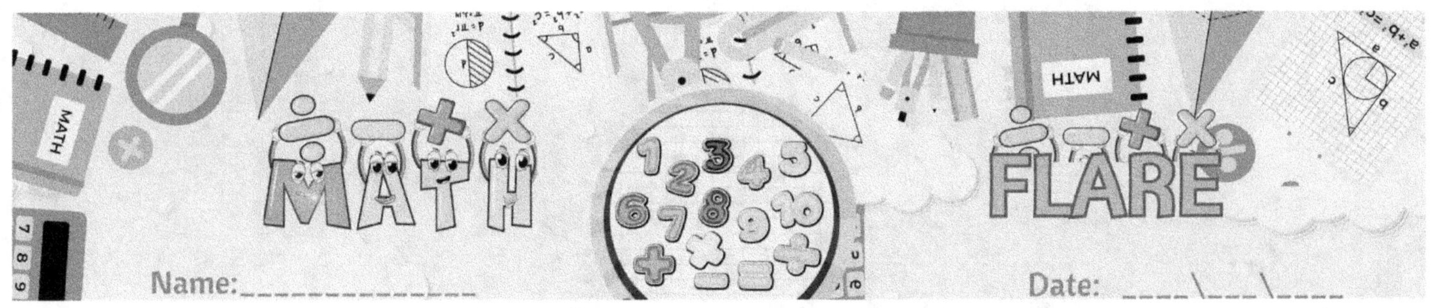

Name:_______________ Date: _______________

108. _______________ 4 thousands + 7 hundreds + 3 tens

109. _______________ 7 thousands + 9 hundreds + 1 ten + 4 ones

110. _______________ 1 thousand + 6 hundreds + 2 tens + 1 one

111. _______________ 7 thousands + 2 hundreds + 6 tens + 9 ones

112. _______________ 4 thousands + 5 hundreds + 2 tens + 7 ones

113. _______________ 3 thousands + 4 hundreds + 6 tens + 1 one

114. _______________ 4 thousands + 3 hundreds + 8 tens

115. _______________ 4 thousands + 4 hundreds + 1 ten + 6 ones

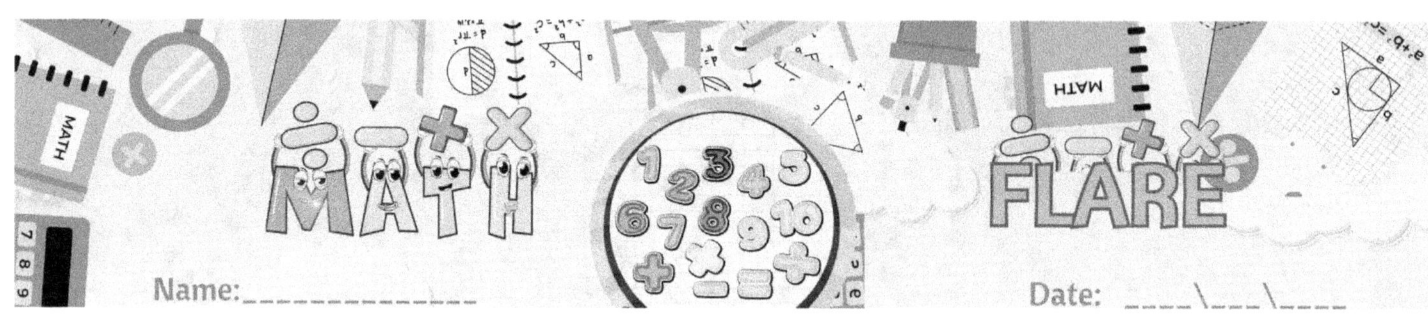

116. _____________ 2 thousands + 9 hundreds + 4 tens + 1 one

117. _____________ 5 thousands + 7 hundreds + 1 ten

118. _____________ 4 thousands + 1 hundred + 1 ten + 6 ones

119. _____________ 4 thousands + 1 hundred + 6 tens + 3 ones

120. _____________ 2 thousands + 2 tens + 2 ones

121. _____________ 2 hundreds + 2 ones

122. _____________ 5 thousands + 9 hundreds + 6 tens + 1 one

123. _____________ 5 thousands + 2 hundreds + 6 tens + 8 ones

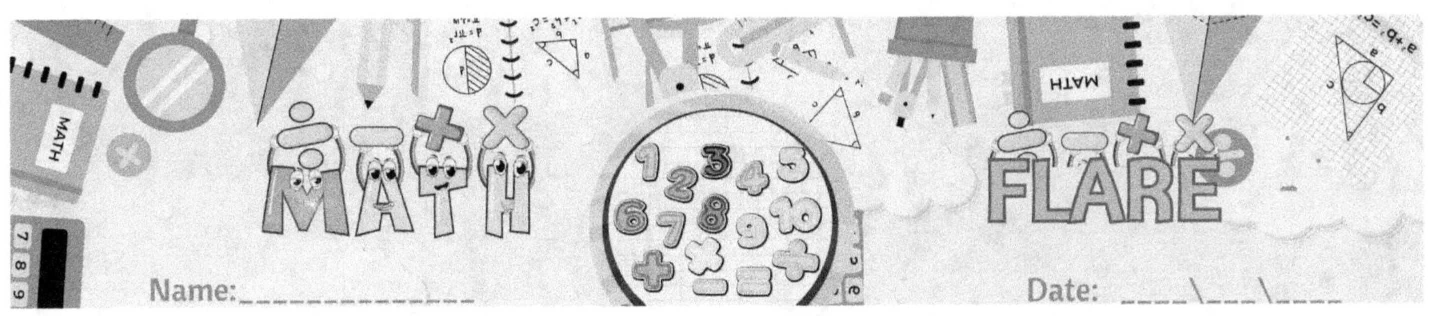

124. _______________ 7 thousands + 5 hundreds + 8 tens + 7 ones

125. _______________ 2 thousands + 2 hundreds + 1 ten + 6 ones

126. _______________ 3 thousands + 5 hundreds + 5 tens + 3 ones

127. _______________ 6 thousands + 1 hundred + 7 ones

128. _______________ 8 thousands + 7 hundreds + 6 tens + 6 ones

129. _______________ 6 thousands + 7 hundreds + 6 tens

130. _______________ 9 thousands + 9 hundreds + 9 tens + 5 ones

131. _______________ 7 thousands + 8 hundreds + 1 ten + 1 one

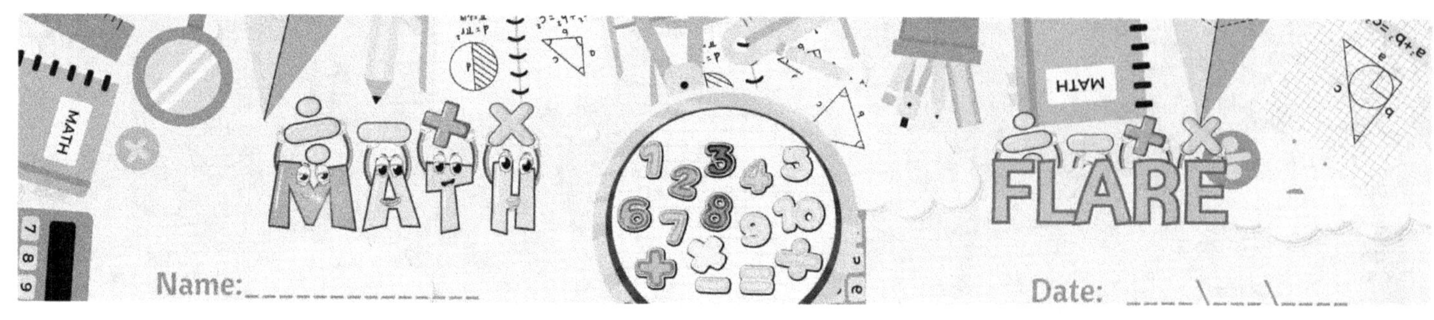

132. _______________ 5 thousands + 7 hundreds + 6 tens + 1 one

133. _______________ 2 thousands + 4 ones

134. _______________ 3 thousands + 8 hundreds + 4 tens + 9 ones

135. _______________ 9 thousands + 6 hundreds + 3 tens

136. _______________ 8 thousands + 9 hundreds + 1 one

137. _______________ 4 hundreds + 9 ones

138. _______________ 4 thousands + 9 hundreds + 5 tens + 5 ones

139. _______________ 6 thousands + 3 hundreds + 7 tens + 1 one

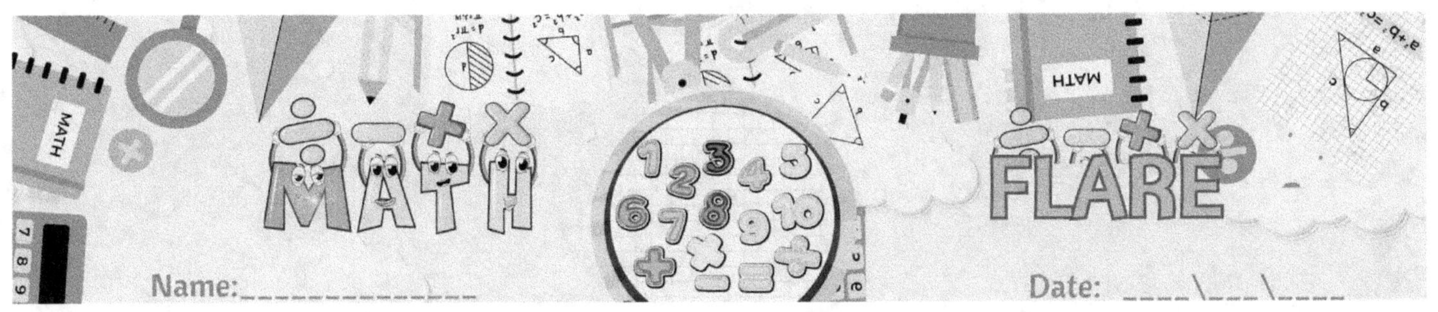

140. _______________ 3 hundreds + 6 tens + 3 ones

141. _______________ 2 thousands + 3 hundreds + 2 tens + 1 one

142. _______________ 7 hundreds + 1 ten + 4 ones

143. _______________ 3 hundreds + 9 tens + 2 ones

144. _______________ 7 thousands + 8 hundreds + 7 tens + 1 one

145. _______________ 4 thousands + 3 hundreds + 9 tens + 9 ones

146. _______________ 3 thousands + 3 tens + 1 one

147. _______________ 6 thousands + 8 tens + 4 ones

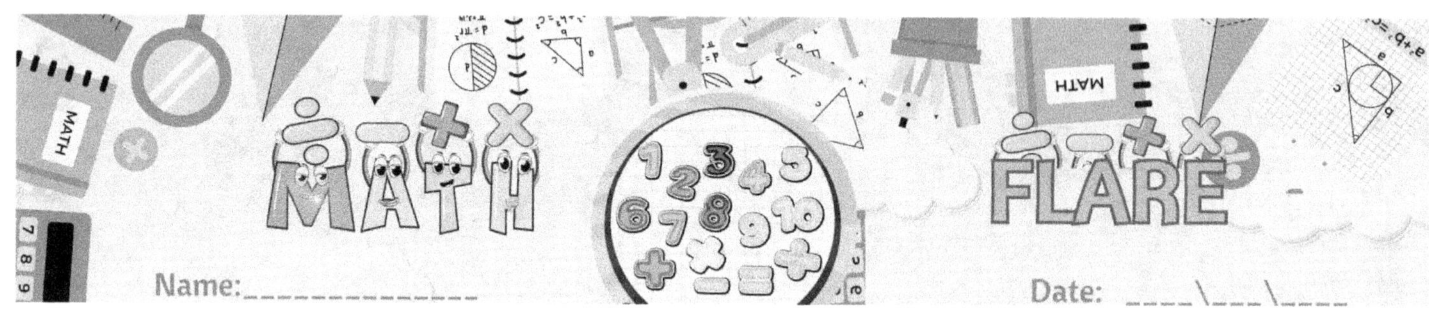

148. __________ 5 thousands + 6 tens + 3 ones

149. __________ 5 thousands + 1 hundred + 9 tens + 2 ones

150. __________ 1 thousand + 8 hundreds + 7 tens + 2 ones

151. __________ 8 thousands + 2 hundreds + 2 ones

152. __________ 3 thousands + 5 hundreds + 1 ten + 5 ones

153. __________ 6 thousands + 5 hundreds + 7 ones

154. __________ 4 thousands + 4 hundreds + 5 tens + 6 ones

155. __________ 7 thousands + 4 hundreds + 7 tens + 6 ones

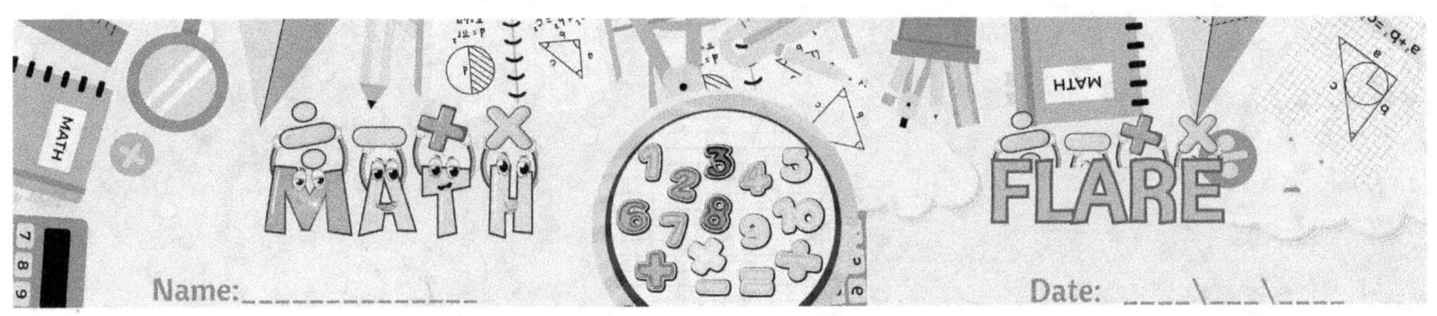

156. __________ 3 thousands + 2 hundreds + 9 tens + 2 ones

157. __________ 7 thousands + 7 hundreds + 3 tens

158. __________ 2 thousands + 8 hundreds + 8 tens + 7 ones

159. __________ 3 hundreds + 7 tens

160. __________ 7 thousands + 9 ones

161. __________ 2 thousands + 7 hundreds + 9 tens + 3 ones

162. __________ 9 thousands + 4 tens + 7 ones

163. __________ 7 thousands + 9 hundreds + 6 tens + 9 ones

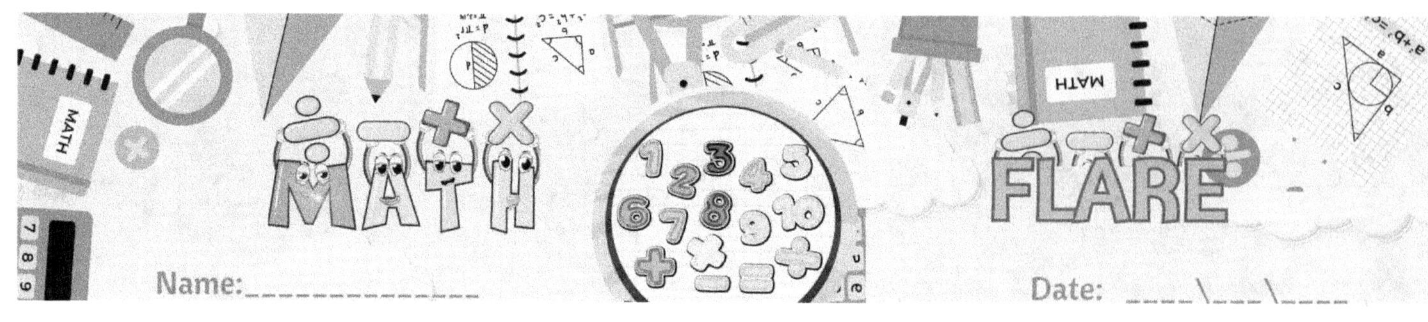

164. _______________ 7 thousands + 9 hundreds + 1 ten + 8 ones

165. _______________ 3 thousands + 8 hundreds + 8 ones

166. _______________ 1 thousand + 5 hundreds + 9 ones

167. _______________ 2 thousands + 5 hundreds + 2 tens + 4 ones

168. _______________ 9 thousands + 6 hundreds + 1 ten + 1 one

169. _______________ 4 thousands + 7 hundreds + 5 tens

170. _______________ 5 thousands + 5 hundreds + 1 ten + 5 ones

171. _______________ 2 thousands + 5 hundreds + 3 tens + 4 ones

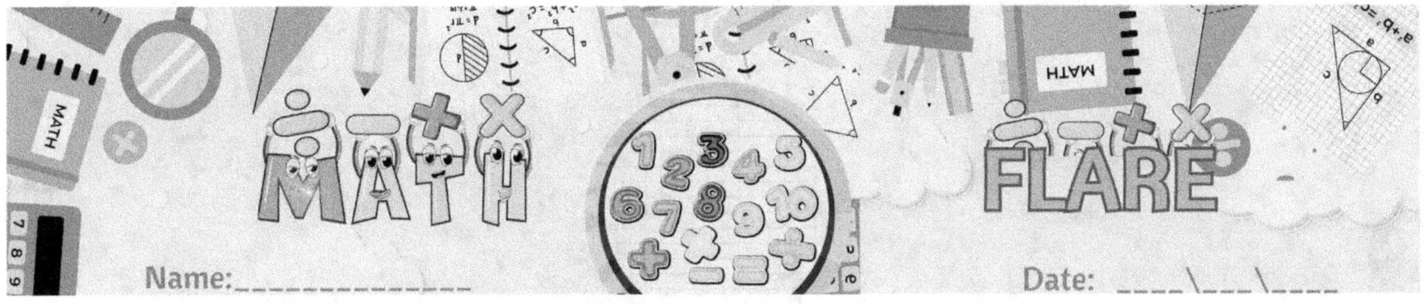

Place Value: Expanded Notation

Provide the expanded notation for each value.

172. 9,700 ___________________

173. 4,162 ___________________

174. 7,876 ___________________

175. 8,218 ___________________

176. 9,736 ___________________

177. 9,359 ___________________

178. 784 ___________________

179. 2,192 ___________________

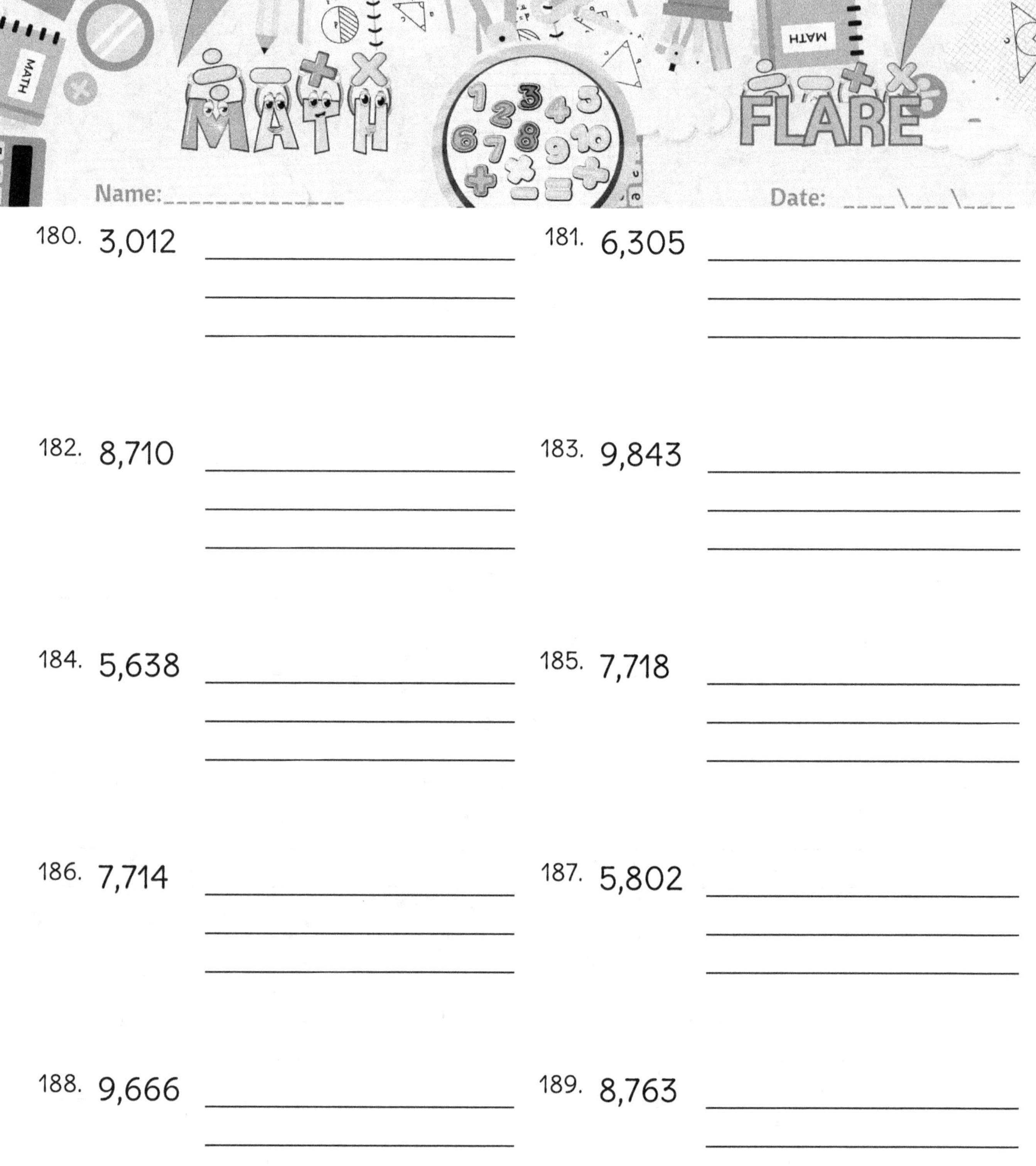

180. 3,012 ___________________
____
____

181. 6,305 ___________________
____
____

182. 8,710 ___________________
____
____

183. 9,843 ___________________
____
____

184. 5,638 ___________________
____
____

185. 7,718 ___________________
____
____

186. 7,714 ___________________
____
____

187. 5,802 ___________________
____
____

188. 9,666 ___________________
____
____

189. 8,763 ___________________
____
____

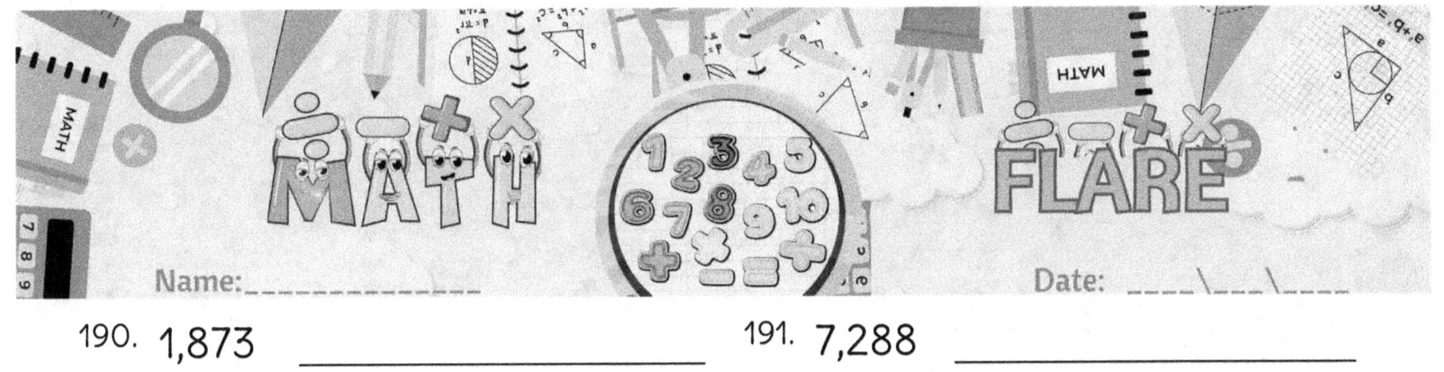

190. 1,873 _______________________

191. 7,288 _______________________

192. 5,606 _______________________

193. 2,402 _______________________

194. 4,948 _______________________

195. 2,180 _______________________

196. 5,212 _______________________

197. 4,737 _______________________

198. 9,798 _______________________

199. 9,385 _______________________

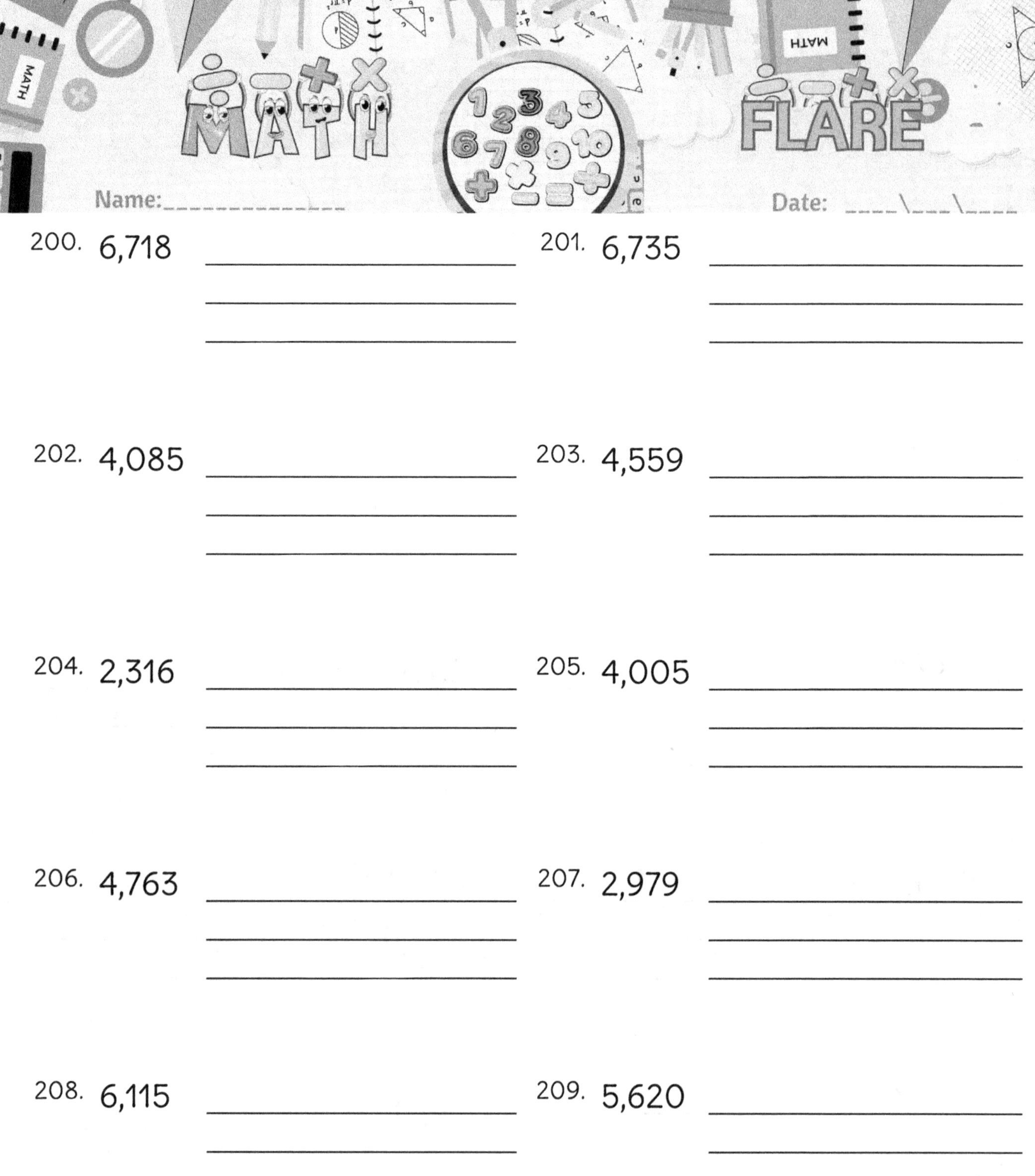

200. 6,718 ___________________

201. 6,735 ___________________

202. 4,085 ___________________

203. 4,559 ___________________

204. 2,316 ___________________

205. 4,005 ___________________

206. 4,763 ___________________

207. 2,979 ___________________

208. 6,115 ___________________

209. 5,620 ___________________

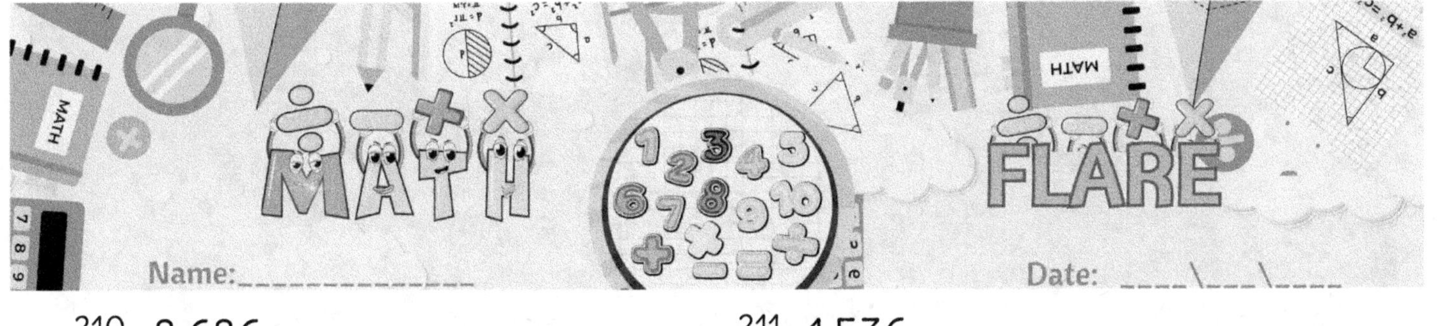

210. 8,686 ______________________

211. 1,536 ______________________

212. 492 ______________________

213. 2,612 ______________________

214. 3,214 ______________________

215. 5,828 ______________________

216. 5,859 ______________________

217. 3,725 ______________________

218. 9,287 ______________________

219. 5,629 ______________________

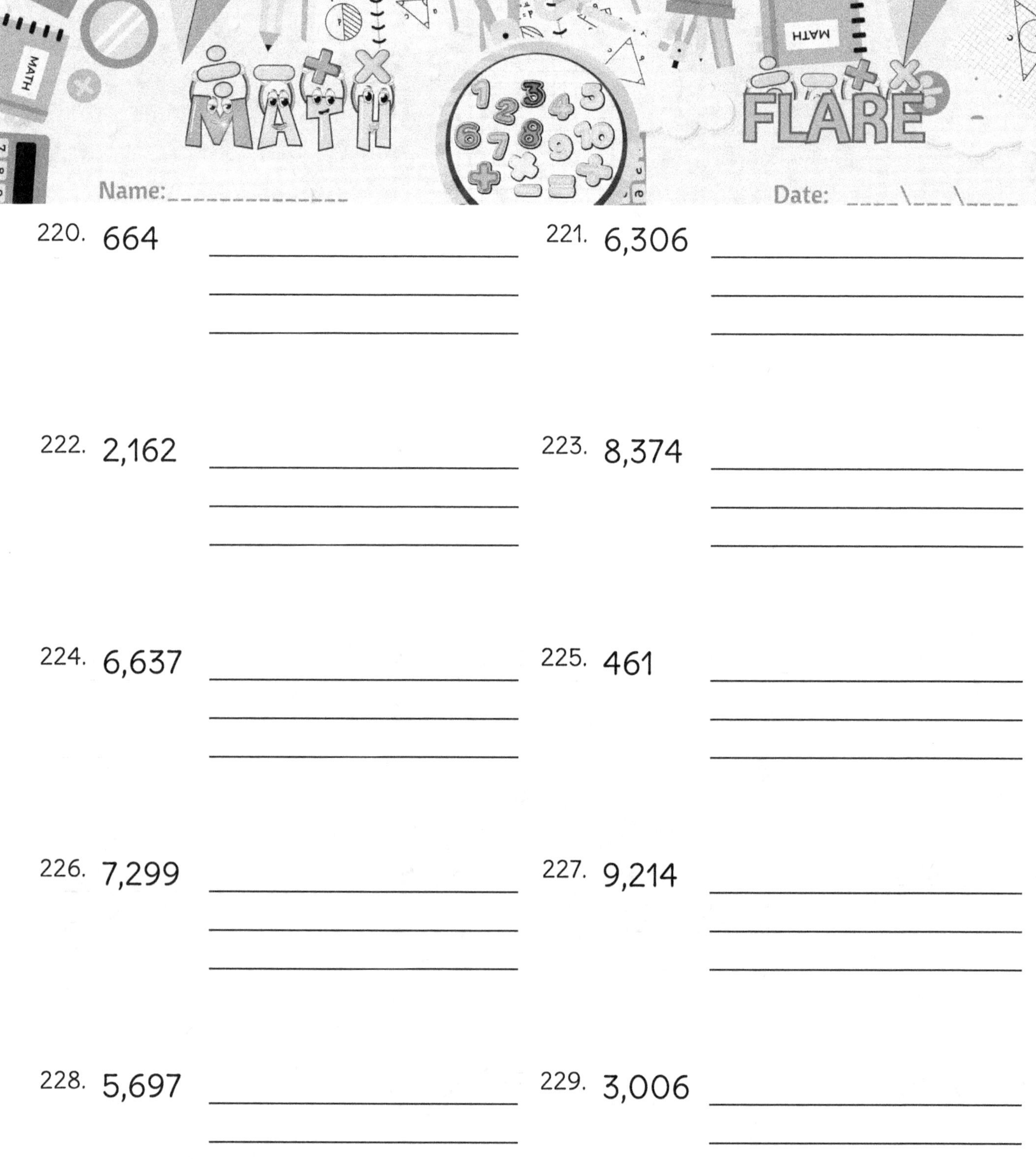

220. 664 _______________

221. 6,306 _______________

222. 2,162 _______________

223. 8,374 _______________

224. 6,637 _______________

225. 461 _______________

226. 7,299 _______________

227. 9,214 _______________

228. 5,697 _______________

229. 3,006 _______________

230. 5,000 _______________________

231. 9,560 _______________________

232. 1,398 _______________________

233. 5,473 _______________________

234. 6,276 _______________________

235. 2,222 _______________________

236. 4,152 _______________________

237. 7,527 _______________________

238. 1,635 _______________________

239. 2,956 _______________________

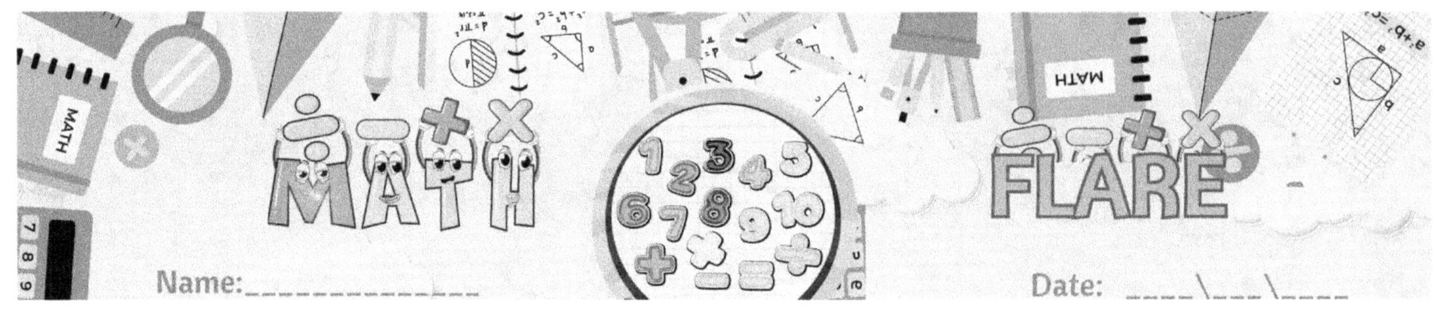

Place Value: Expanded Notation

Provide the expanded notation for each value.

240. _____________ 3,000 + 800 + 50 + 3

241. _____________ 2,000 + 200 + 50 + 8

242. _____________ 7,000 + 900 + 40 + 4

243. _____________ 7,000 + 600 + 8

244. _____________ 6,000 + 400 + 20 + 7

245. _____________ 3,000 + 300 + 20 + 5

246. _____________ 9,000 + 900 + 30 + 2

247. _____________ 9,000 + 200 + 70 + 7

248. _____________ 9,000 + 200 + 10 + 5

249. _____________ 5,000 + 100 + 30 + 8

250. _____________ 4,000 + 300 + 50 + 1

251. _____________ 7,000 + 200

252. _____________ 1,000 + 700 + 50 + 1

253. _____________ 6,000 + 400 + 20 + 3

254. _____________ 1,000 + 80 + 3

255. _____________ 2,000 + 200 + 90 + 2

256. _____________ 9,000 + 20 + 6

257. _____________ 4,000 + 100 + 30 + 8

258. _____________ 3,000 + 300 + 80 + 1

259. _____________ 7,000 + 800 + 50 + 3

260. _____________ 9,000 + 900 + 50 + 3

261. _____________ 6,000 + 400 + 60 + 5

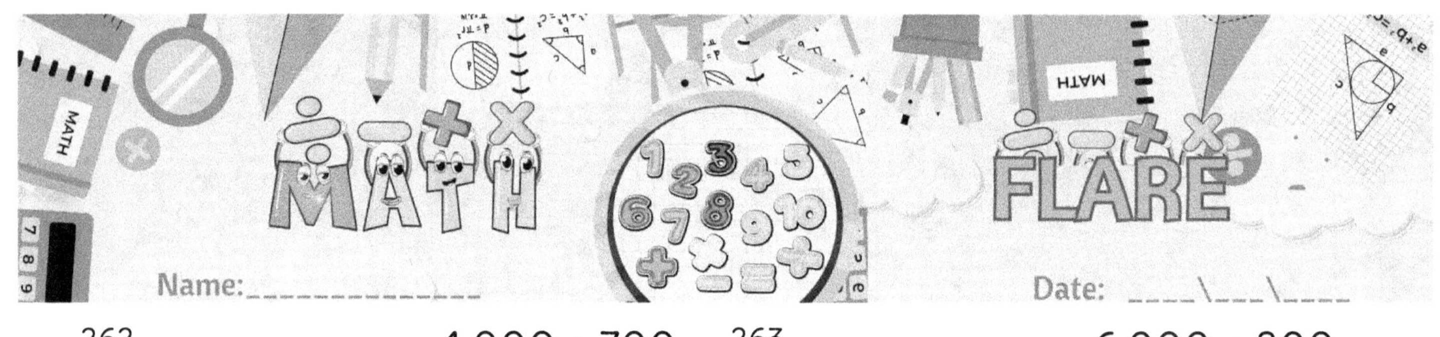

262. __________ 4,000 + 700 + 80 + 1

263. __________ 6,000 + 800 + 10 + 6

264. __________ 9,000 + 200 + 50 + 6

265. __________ 1,000 + 300 + 9

266. __________ 1,000 + 200 + 6

267. __________ 8,000 + 500 + 20 + 4

268. __________ 9,000 + 500 + 90 + 9

269. __________ 2,000 + 70 + 6

270. __________ 2,000 + 400 + 9

271. __________ 8,000 + 9

272. __________ 6,000 + 200 + 10 + 1

273. __________ 400 + 60 + 4

274. __________ 1,000 + 200 + 40 + 6

275. __________ 8,000 + 600 + 70 + 6

276. __________ 600 + 6

277. __________ 8,000 + 300 + 6

278. __________ 8,000 + 600 + 1

279. __________ 2,000 + 200 + 60 + 9

280. __________ 6,000 + 100 + 90 + 2

281. __________ 2,000 + 200 + 30 + 4

282. __________ 7,000 + 200 + 50 + 7

283. __________ 3,000 + 900 + 80 + 8

284. __________ 9,000 + 100 + 30 + 8

285. __________ 400 + 20 + 9

286. __________ 4,000 + 100 + 4

287. __________ 7,000 + 500 + 70 + 1

288. __________ 200 + 5

289. __________ 4,000 + 800 + 80 + 3

290. __________ 7,000 + 400 + 8

291. __________ 2,000 + 100 + 90 + 2

292. __________ 1,000 + 800 + 6

293. __________ 8,000 + 100 + 90

294. __________ 3,000 + 200 + 20 + 5

295. __________ 7,000 + 300 + 80 + 7

296. __________ 7,000 + 400 + 70 + 6

297. __________ 1,000 + 100 + 30

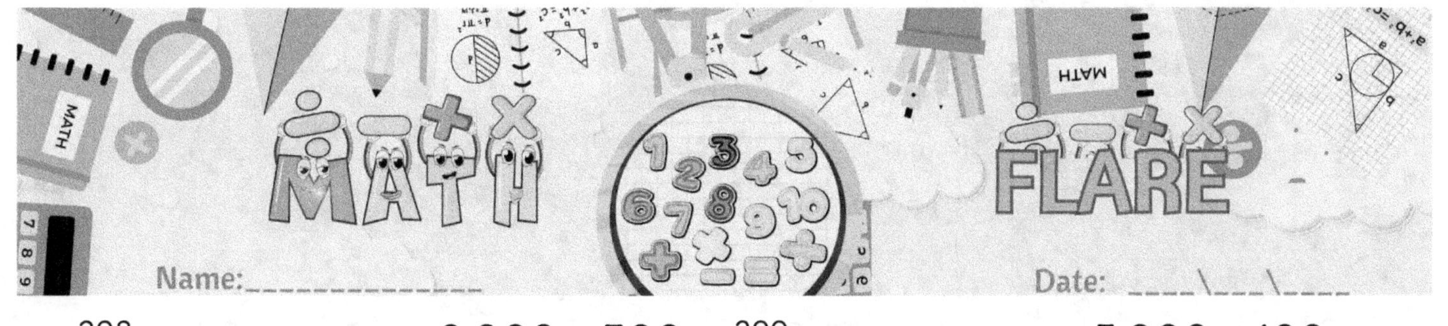

298. _____________ 8,000 + 300 + 50 + 1

299. _____________ 5,000 + 100 + 10 + 9

300. _____________ 2,000 + 100 + 20

301. _____________ 1,000 + 400 + 10

302. _____________ 9,000 + 600 + 70 + 8

303. _____________ 7,000 + 100 + 40

304. _____________ 2,000 + 700 + 30

305. _____________ 6,000 + 300 + 40 + 1

306. _____________ 900 + 90

307. _____________ 1,000 + 200 + 80 + 8

308. _____________ 5,000 + 100 + 70 + 8

309. _____________ 2,000 + 400 + 7

310. _______________ 1,000 + 600 + 80 + 7

311. _______________ 700 + 20

312. _______________ 5,000 + 500 + 30 + 6

313. _______________ 1,000 + 100 + 10 + 3

314. _______________ 1,000 + 600 + 60 + 2

315. _______________ 7,000 + 700 + 20

316. _______________ 9,000 + 200 + 7

317. _______________ 700 + 90 + 4

318. _______________ 7,000 + 600 + 70 + 7

319. _______________ 8,000 + 800 + 20 + 8

320. _______________ 7,000 + 200 + 4

321. _______________ 3,000 + 600 + 30 + 3

Place Value: Expanded Notation

Provide the expanded notation for each value.

322. 8,319 _______________________

323. 4,716 _______________________

324. 4,667 _______________________

325. 218 _______________________

326. 6,204 _______________________

327. 8,020 _______________________

328. 7,238 _______________________

329. 3,858 _______________________

330. 1,201 _______________________

331. 9,475 _______________________

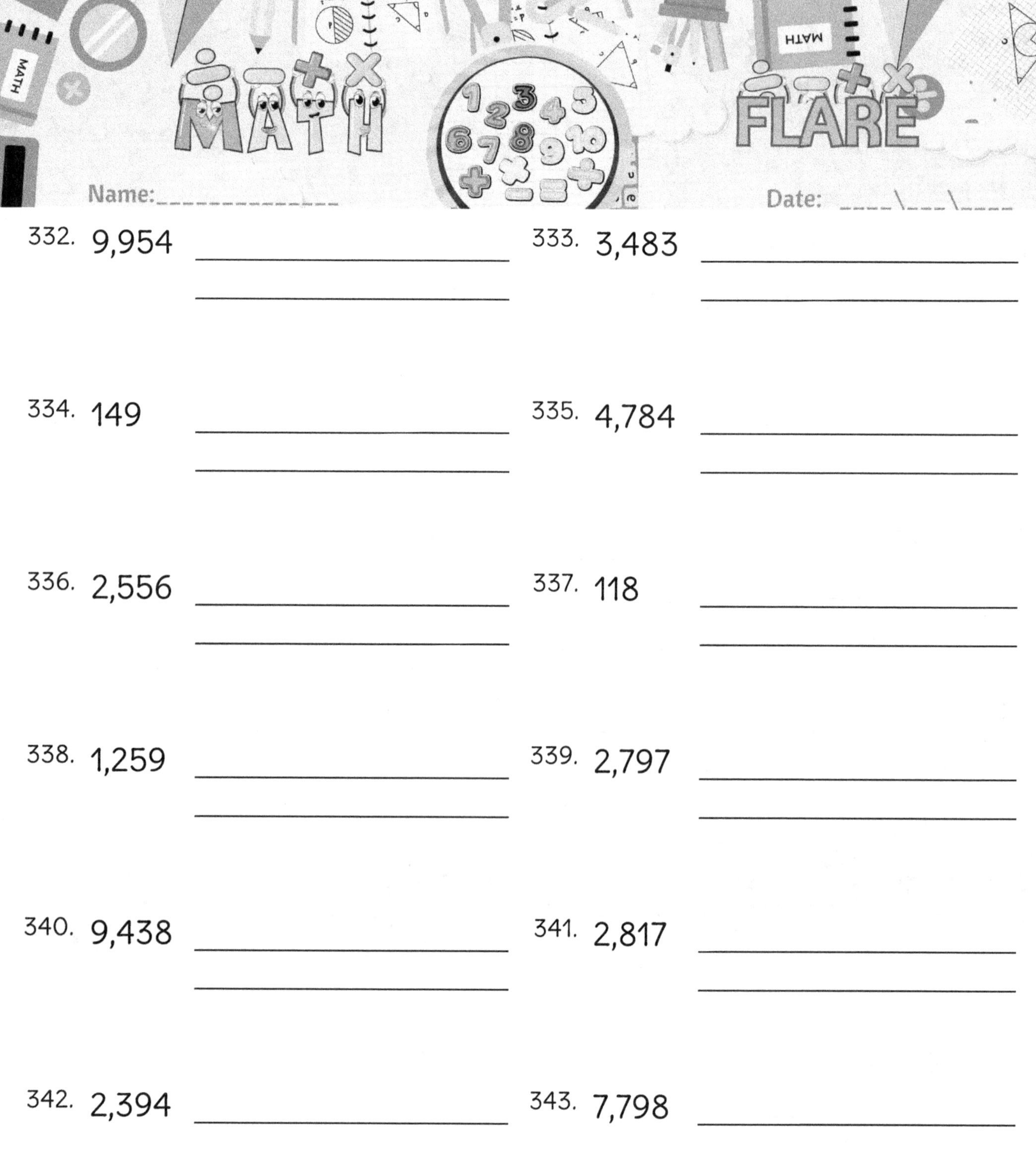

Name:_______________   Date: _______________

332. 9,954 _______________________
____

333. 3,483 _______________________
____

334. 149 _______________________
____

335. 4,784 _______________________
____

336. 2,556 _______________________
____

337. 118 _______________________
____

338. 1,259 _______________________
____

339. 2,797 _______________________
____

340. 9,438 _______________________
____

341. 2,817 _______________________
____

342. 2,394 _______________________
____

343. 7,798 _______________________
____

344. 3,197 ______________________

345. 6,688 ______________________

346. 6,655 ______________________

347. 694 ______________________

348. 6,529 ______________________

349. 5,504 ______________________

350. 8,179 ______________________

351. 6,683 ______________________

352. 3,452 ______________________

353. 9,522 ______________________

354. 7,914 ______________________

355. 8,486 ______________________

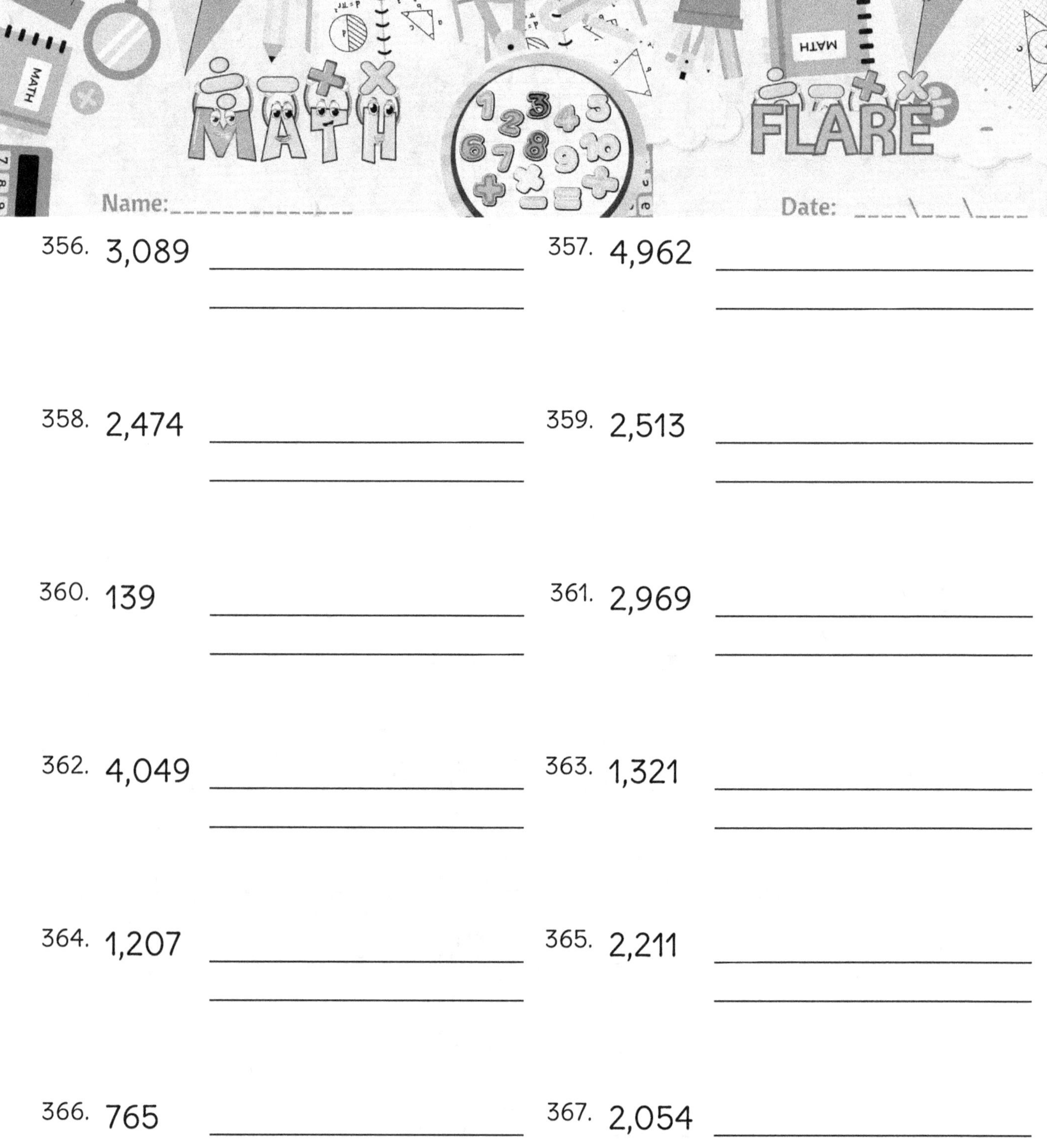

356. 3,089 ________________________
____

357. 4,962 ________________________
____

358. 2,474 ________________________
____

359. 2,513 ________________________
____

360. 139 ________________________
____

361. 2,969 ________________________
____

362. 4,049 ________________________
____

363. 1,321 ________________________
____

364. 1,207 ________________________
____

365. 2,211 ________________________
____

366. 765 ________________________
____

367. 2,054 ________________________
____

368. 965 _______________

369. 6,877 _______________

370. 5,166 _______________

371. 9,090 _______________

372. 9,534 _______________

373. 4,880 _______________

374. 9,389 _______________

375. 4,387 _______________

376. 1,240 _______________

377. 522 _______________

378. 1,520 _______________

379. 7,978 _______________

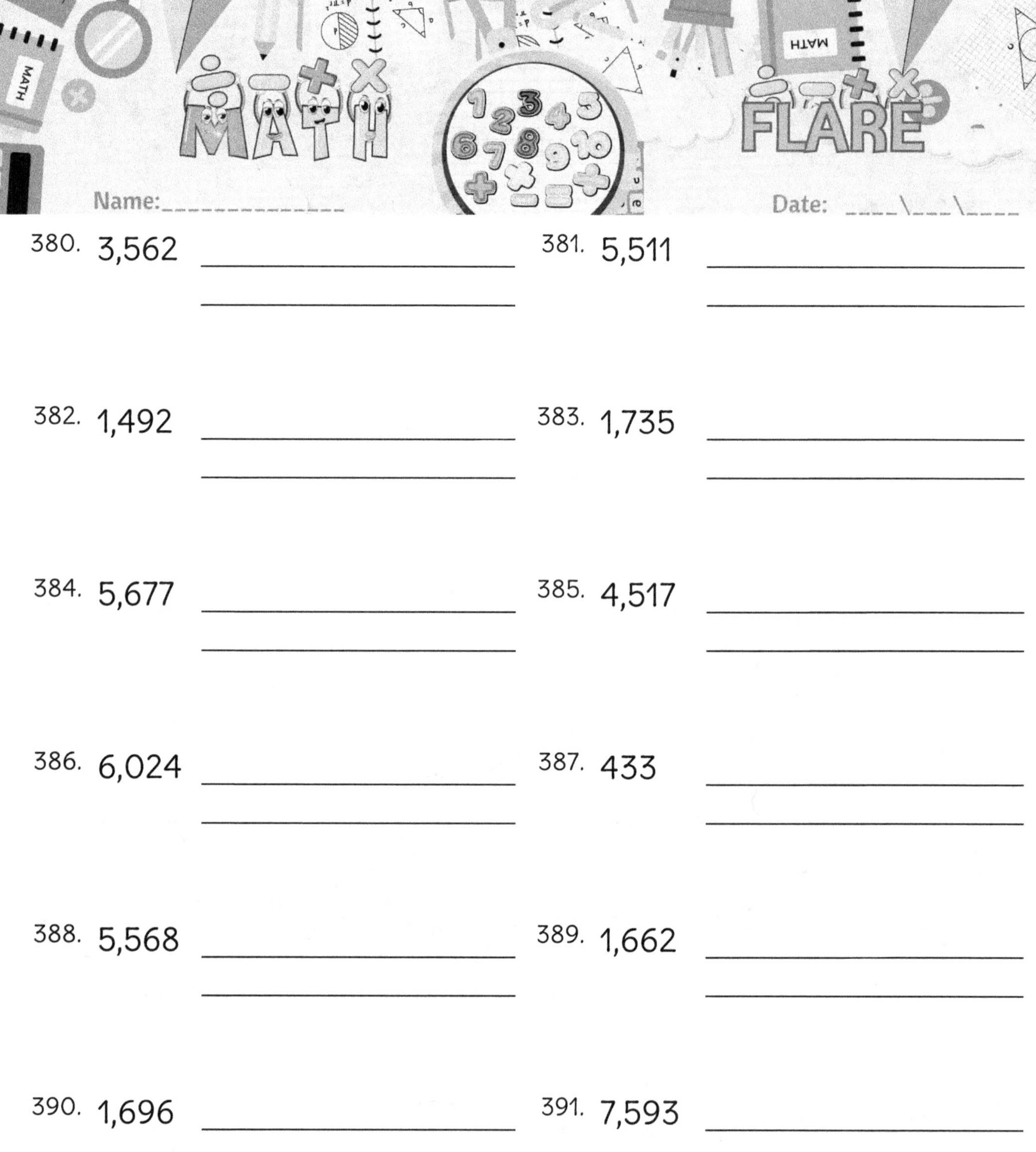

380. 3,562 ___________________

381. 5,511 ___________________

382. 1,492 ___________________

383. 1,735 ___________________

384. 5,677 ___________________

385. 4,517 ___________________

386. 6,024 ___________________

387. 433 ___________________

388. 5,568 ___________________

389. 1,662 ___________________

390. 1,696 ___________________

391. 7,593 ___________________

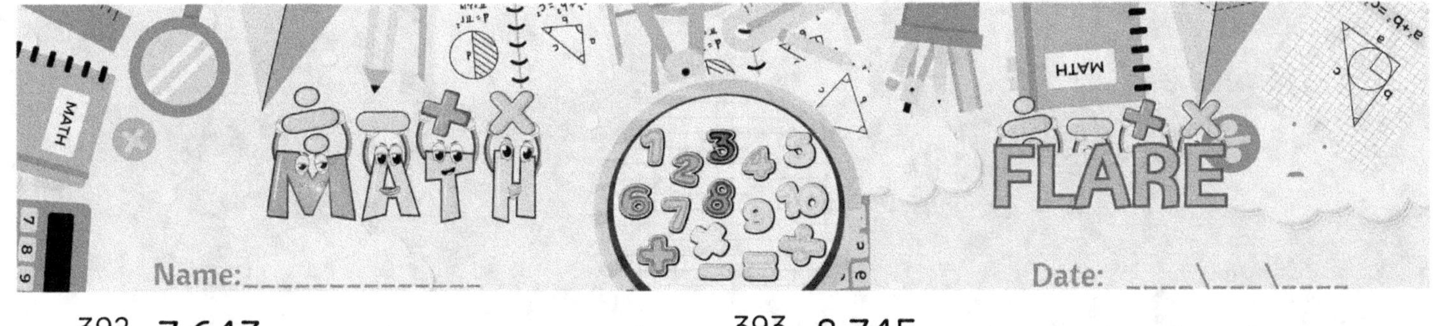

392. 7,643 _______________

393. 8,745 _______________

394. 2,660 _______________

395. 6,470 _______________

396. 8,767 _______________

397. 1,074 _______________

398. 6,592 _______________

399. 988 _______________

400. 5,924 _______________

401. 4,602 _______________

402. 9,728 _______________

403. 9,651 _______________

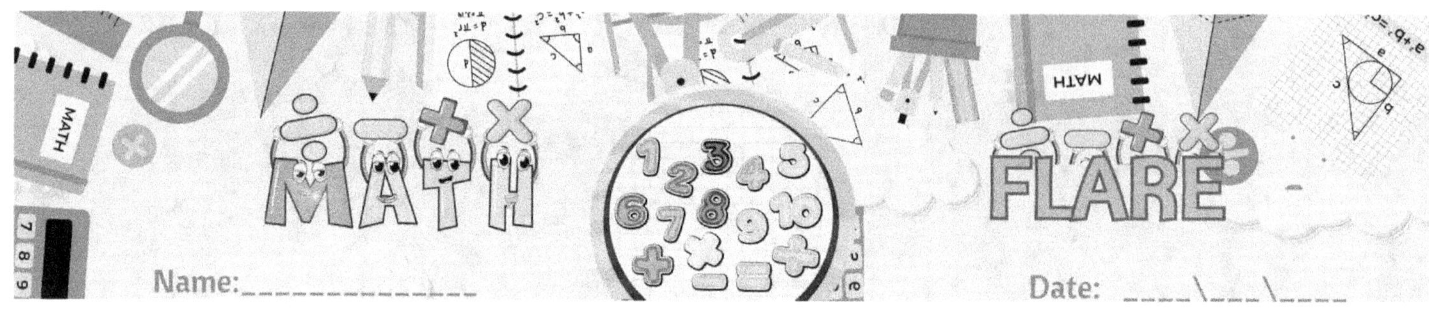

Place Value: Expanded Notation

Provide the expanded notation for each value.

404. _______________ three hundred forty

405. _______________ nine thousand eighty-eight

406. _______________ seven thousand one hundred forty-eight

407. _______________ eight thousand five hundred seventy-one

408. _______________ one hundred thirty-four

409. _______________ three thousand five hundred twenty-eight

410. _______________ seven thousand two hundred forty-seven

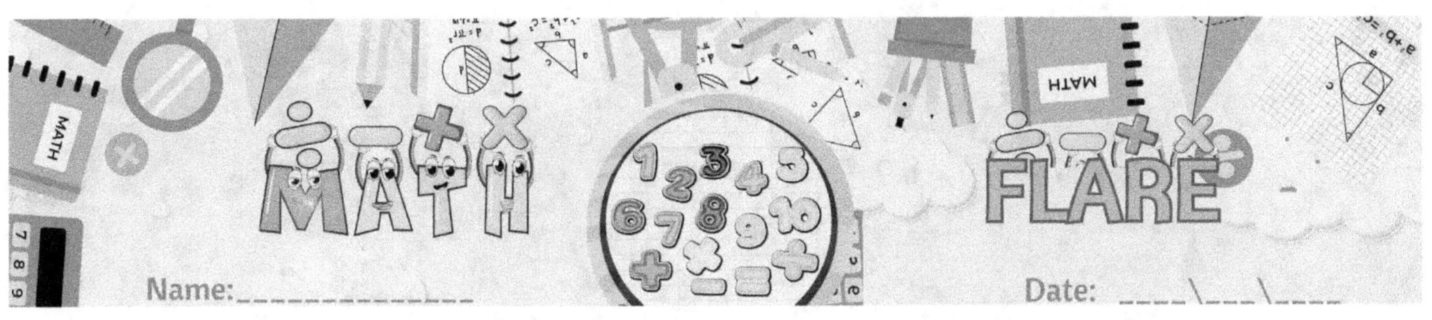

411. _______________ two thousand five hundred sixty-eight

412. _______________ three thousand four hundred forty-three

413. _______________ four thousand four hundred ninety-five

414. _______________ eight thousand nine hundred fifty

415. _______________ four thousand six hundred twenty-seven

416. _______________ one thousand four hundred seventy-eight

417. _______________ two thousand three hundred fifteen

418. _______________ five thousand six hundred forty-three

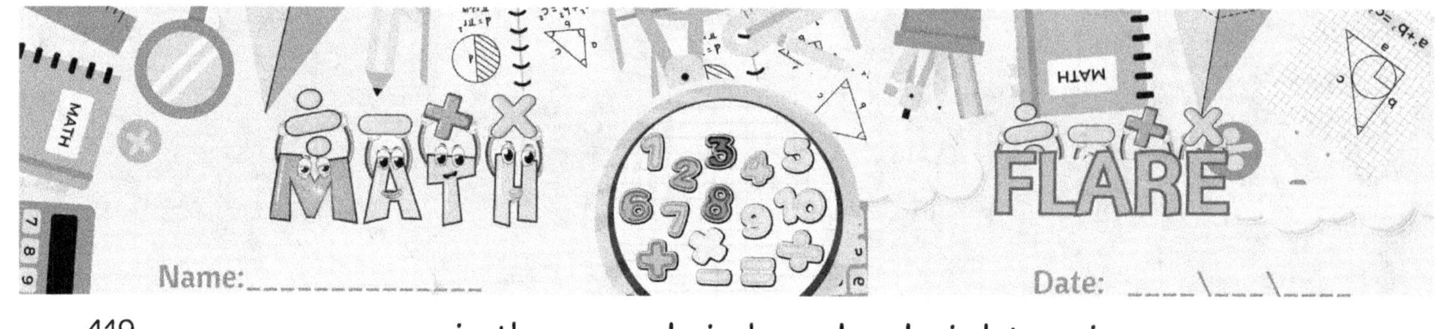

419. __________ six thousand six hundred eighty-nine

420. __________ six thousand one hundred eighty-six

421. __________ three hundred thirty-four

422. __________ six thousand four hundred eighty-five

423. __________ nine thousand three hundred one

424. __________ five thousand one hundred eighty-three

425. __________ seven thousand five hundred seventy-two

426. __________ one thousand four hundred forty-eight

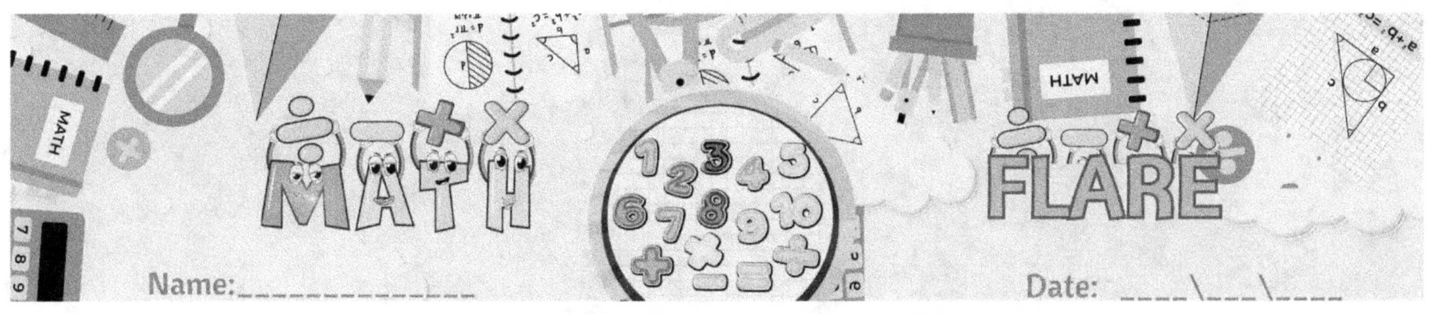

427. ______________ seven hundred ninety

428. ______________ two thousand two hundred twenty-one

429. ______________ two thousand nine hundred twenty

430. ______________ five thousand six hundred nineteen

431. ______________ one hundred sixty-seven

432. ______________ three thousand nine hundred twenty-nine

433. ______________ five hundred thirty-three

434. ______________ two thousand fifty-five

435. _______________ eight thousand nine hundred fifty-nine

436. _______________ five thousand seven hundred eighty-two

437. _______________ one thousand eight hundred forty

438. _______________ one thousand three hundred ninety-six

439. _______________ six thousand five hundred eighty-eight

440. _______________ seven thousand three hundred sixty-eight

441. _______________ seven thousand four hundred fifty-two

442. _______________ two hundred ninety-nine

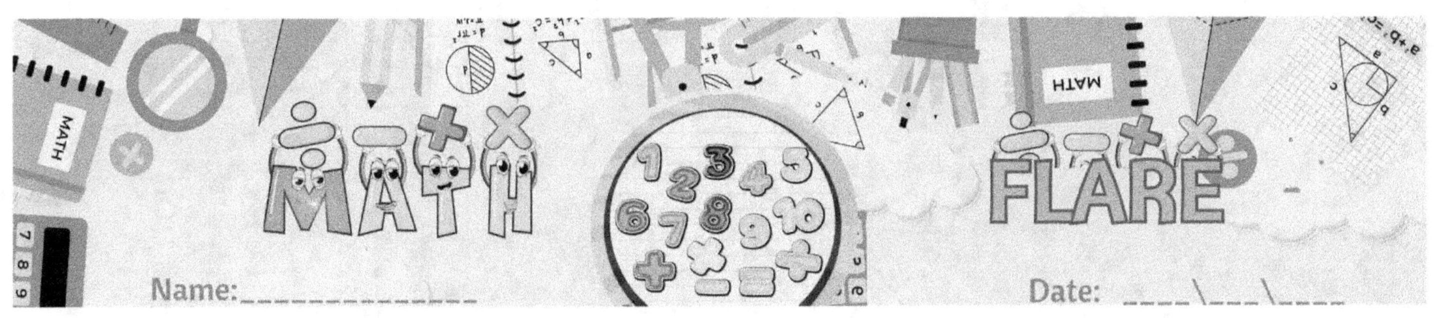

443. _______________ two thousand forty

444. _______________ four thousand four hundred fifteen

445. _______________ nine thousand one hundred twenty-seven

446. _______________ four thousand one hundred fifty-one

447. _______________ three thousand one hundred forty-eight

448. _______________ nine thousand seven hundred ninety-five

449. _______________ eight thousand thirty-two

450. _______________ four thousand nine hundred ninety-four

451. ______________ six thousand four hundred fifty-three

452. ______________ five thousand four hundred thirty

453. ______________ nine thousand nine hundred two

454. ______________ four thousand eight hundred one

455. ______________ five thousand five hundred ninety-one

456. ______________ eight thousand one hundred sixteen

457. ______________ four hundred twenty-seven

458. ______________ four thousand four hundred sixty-nine

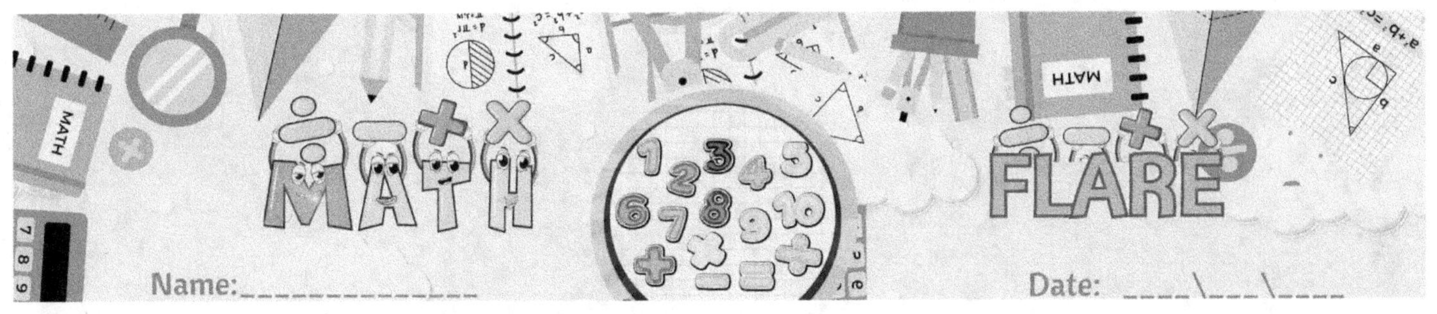

459. _____________ two thousand seven hundred sixty-seven

460. _____________ seven thousand six hundred forty-one

461. _____________ six thousand three hundred fifty-nine

462. _____________ six thousand three hundred fifty

463. _____________ seven thousand two hundred fourteen

464. _____________ seven thousand nine hundred eight

465. _____________ seven thousand eighty

466. _____________ eight thousand six hundred thirty-eight

467. _______________ two thousand nine hundred ten

468. _______________ two thousand four hundred forty-one

469. _______________ nine thousand nine hundred ninety

470. _______________ eight thousand eight hundred forty-three

471. _______________ nine thousand six hundred thirty-six

472. _______________ nine hundred twenty

473. _______________ nine thousand fifty-four

474. _______________ nine thousand three hundred twenty

475. _____________ eight thousand seven hundred thirty-two

476. _____________ thirty-six

477. _____________ four thousand four hundred forty-six

478. _____________ four thousand eight hundred eighty-eight

479. _____________ six thousand fifty-five

480. _____________ three thousand four hundred twenty-two

481. _____________ eight thousand two hundred ninety-nine

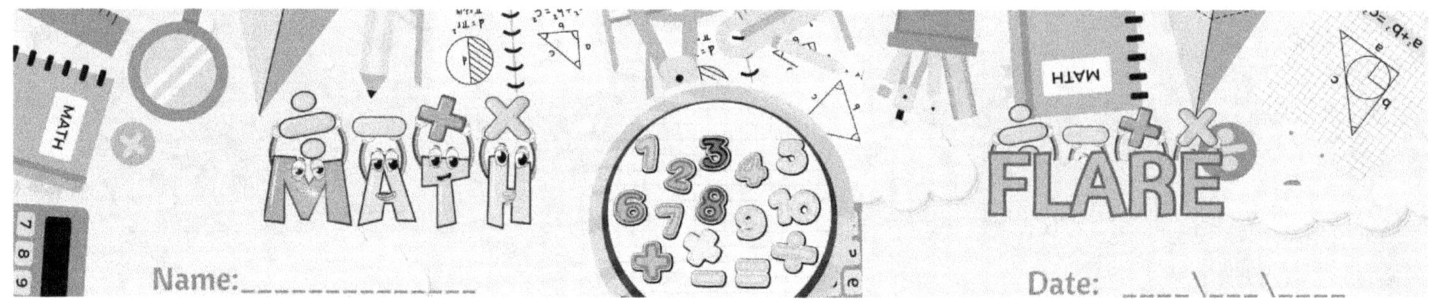

Place Value: Expanded Notation

Provide the expanded notation for each value.

482. 100 _______________________

483. 419 _______________________

484. 792 _______________________

485. 916 _______________________

486. 474 _______________________

487. 403 _______________________

488. 573 _______________________

489. 646 _______________________

490. 85 _______________________

491. 536 _______________________

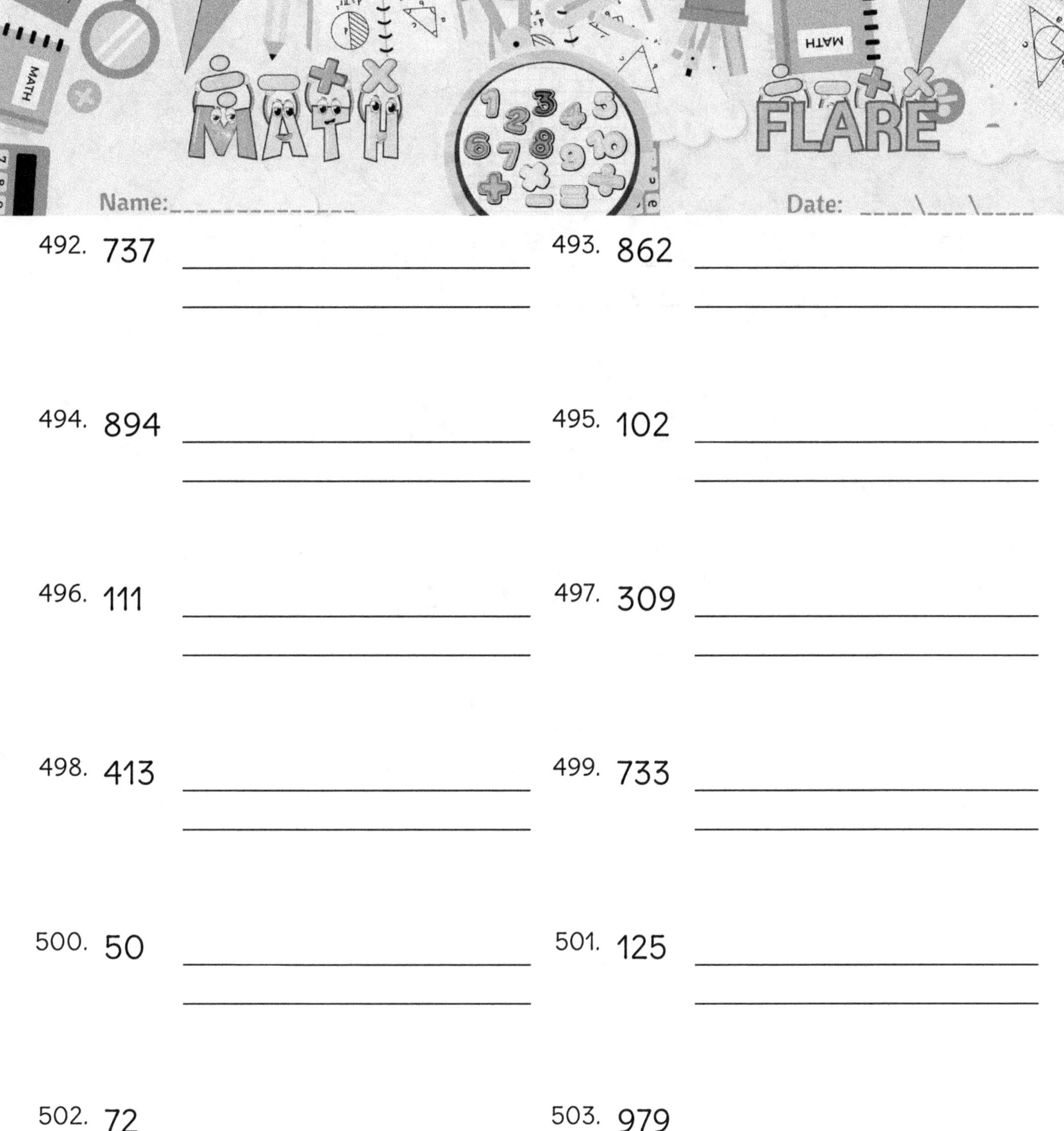

492. 737 __________________________

493. 862 __________________________

494. 894 __________________________

495. 102 __________________________

496. 111 __________________________

497. 309 __________________________

498. 413 __________________________

499. 733 __________________________

500. 50 __________________________

501. 125 __________________________

502. 72 __________________________

503. 979 __________________________

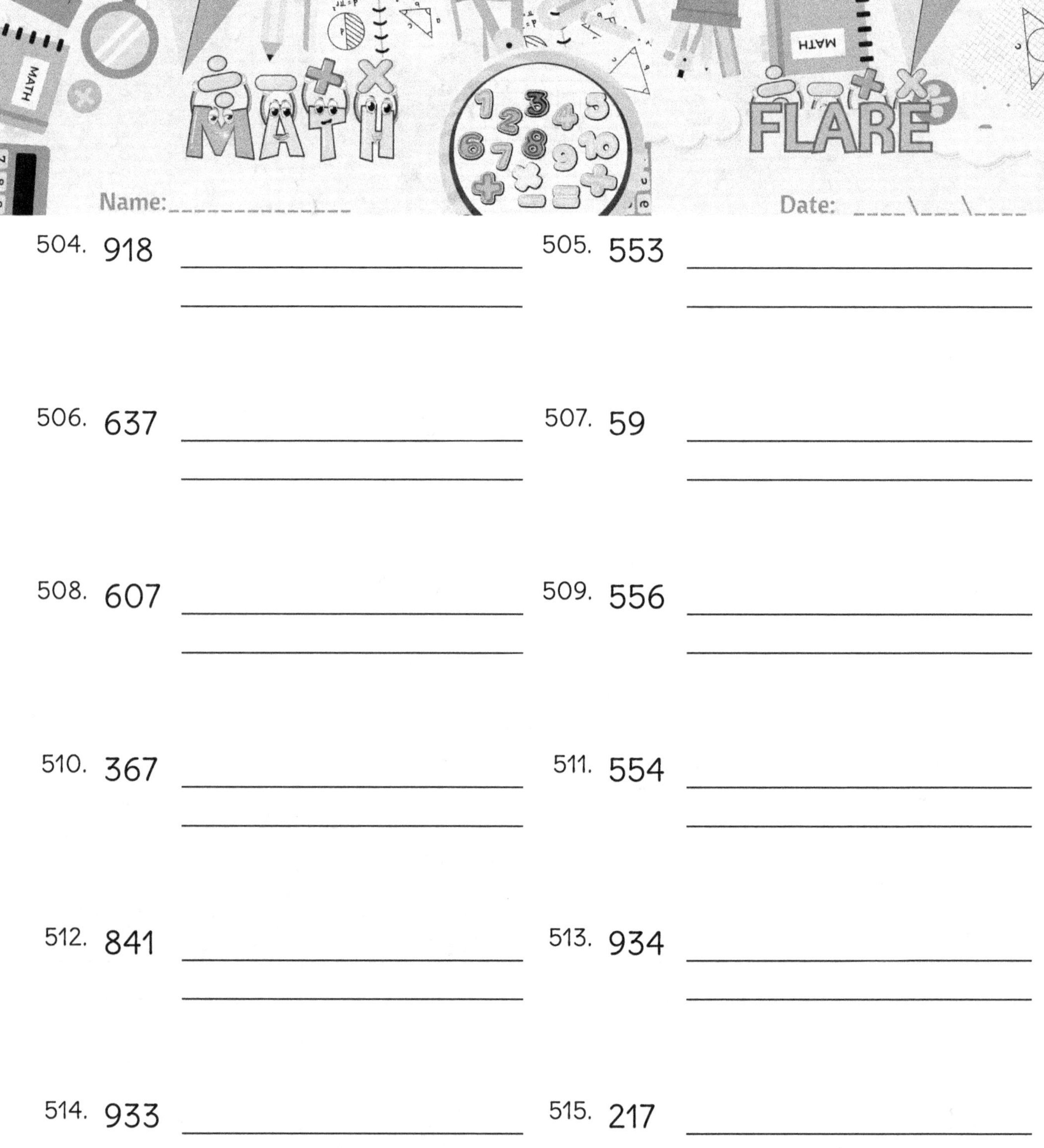

504. 918 __________________

505. 553 __________________

506. 637 __________________

507. 59 __________________

508. 607 __________________

509. 556 __________________

510. 367 __________________

511. 554 __________________

512. 841 __________________

513. 934 __________________

514. 933 __________________

515. 217 __________________

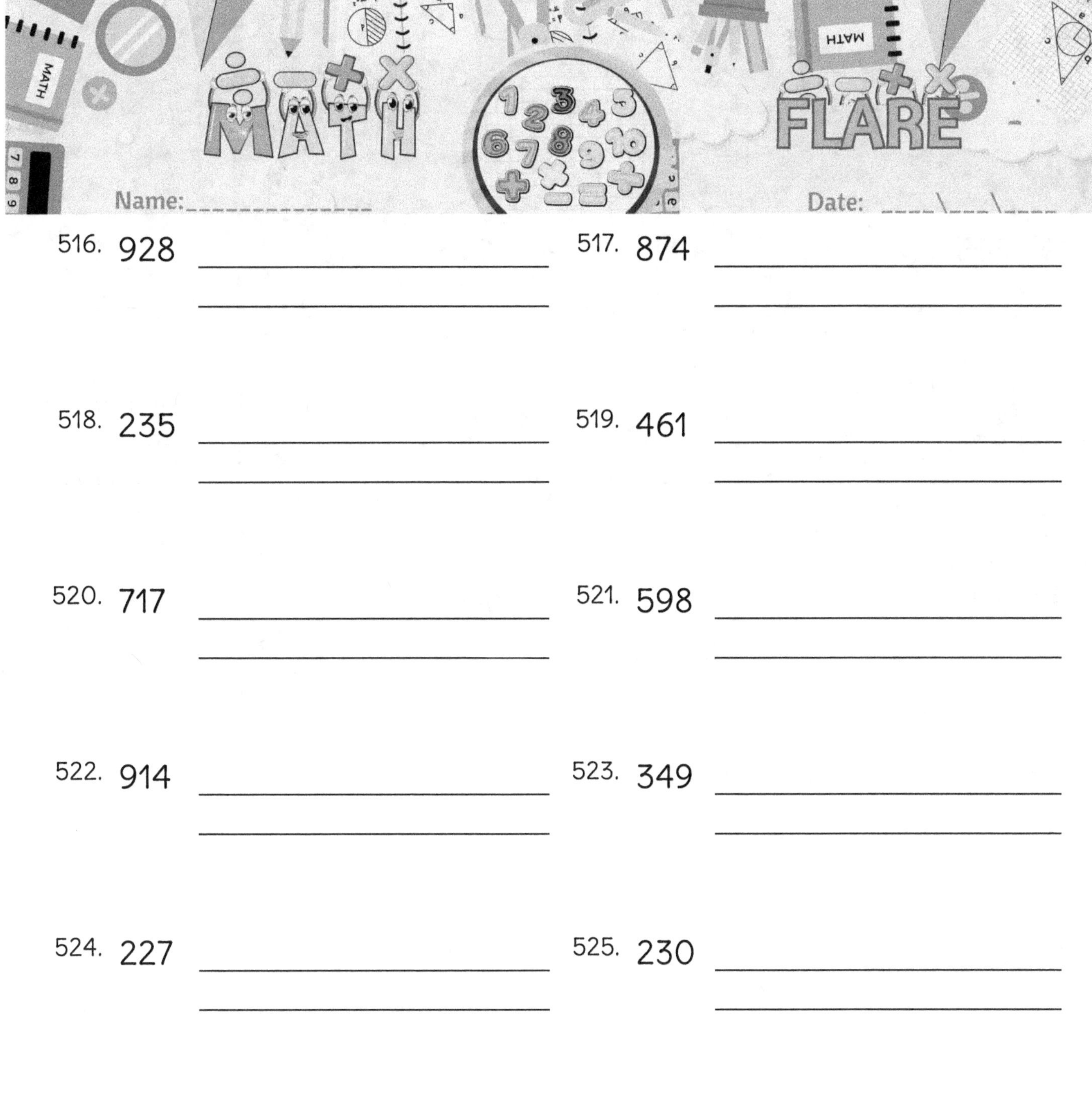

516. 928 __________________

517. 874 __________________

518. 235 __________________

519. 461 __________________

520. 717 __________________

521. 598 __________________

522. 914 __________________

523. 349 __________________

524. 227 __________________

525. 230 __________________

526. 12 __________________

527. 830 __________________

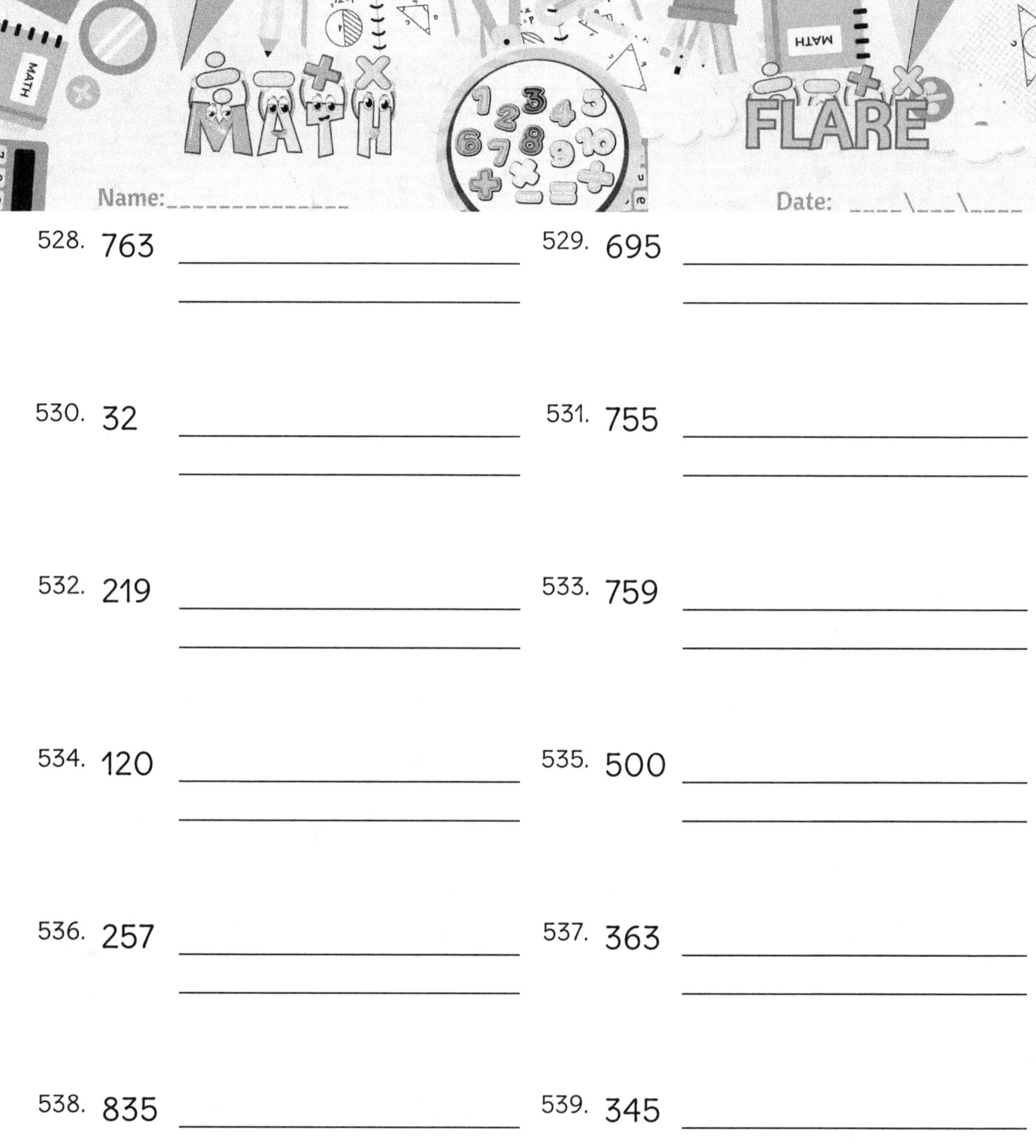

528. 763 ____________________

529. 695 ____________________

530. 32 ____________________

531. 755 ____________________

532. 219 ____________________

533. 759 ____________________

534. 120 ____________________

535. 500 ____________________

536. 257 ____________________

537. 363 ____________________

538. 835 ____________________

539. 345 ____________________

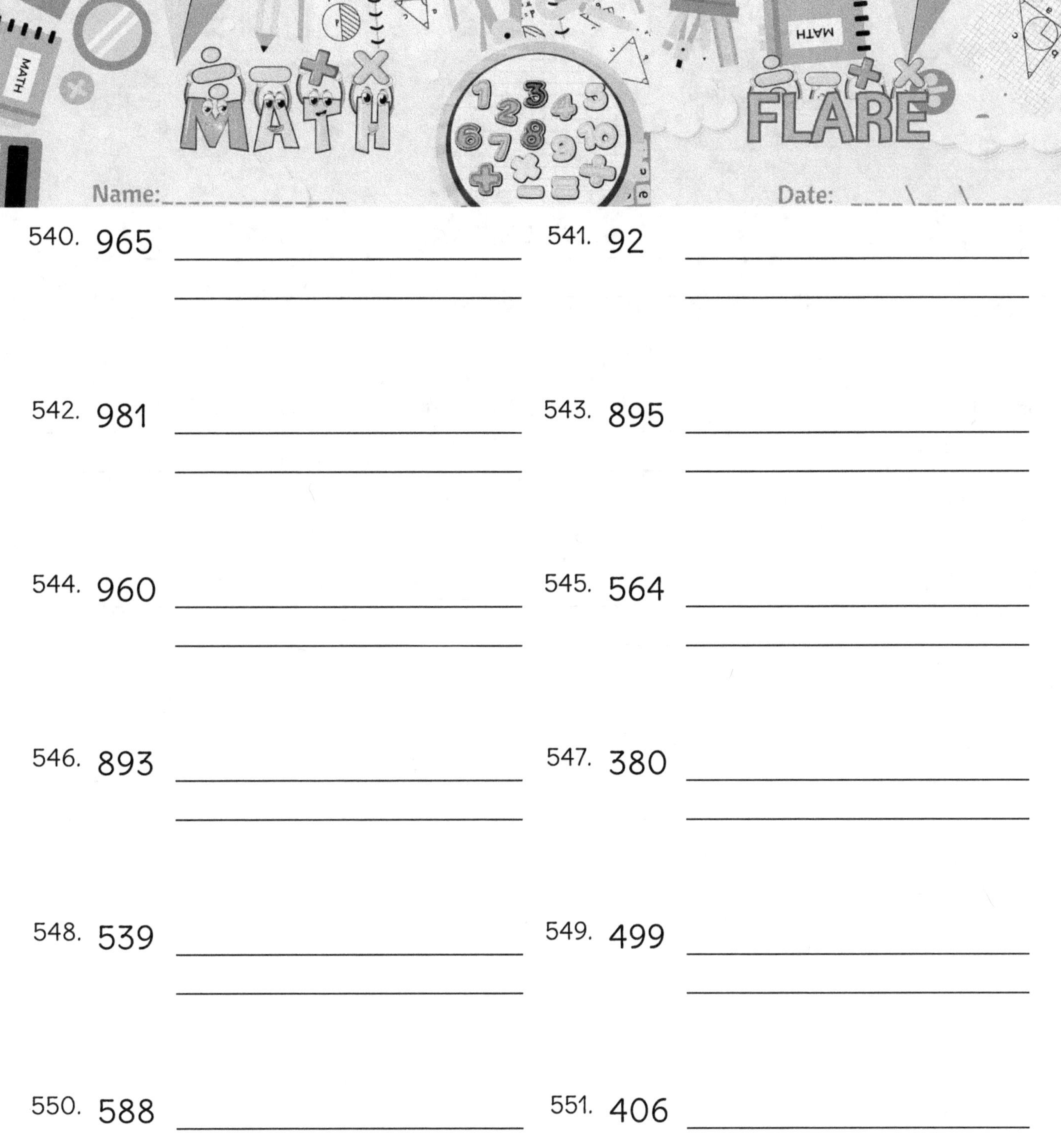

Name: _______________ Date: ____________

540. 965 _______________

541. 92 _______________

542. 981 _______________

543. 895 _______________

544. 960 _______________

545. 564 _______________

546. 893 _______________

547. 380 _______________

548. 539 _______________

549. 499 _______________

550. 588 _______________

551. 406 _______________

552. 473 ___________________

553. 66 ___________________

554. 570 ___________________

555. 325 ___________________

556. 626 ___________________

557. 228 ___________________

558. 843 ___________________

559. 860 ___________________

560. 336 ___________________

561. 798 ___________________

562. 285 ___________________

563. 716 ___________________

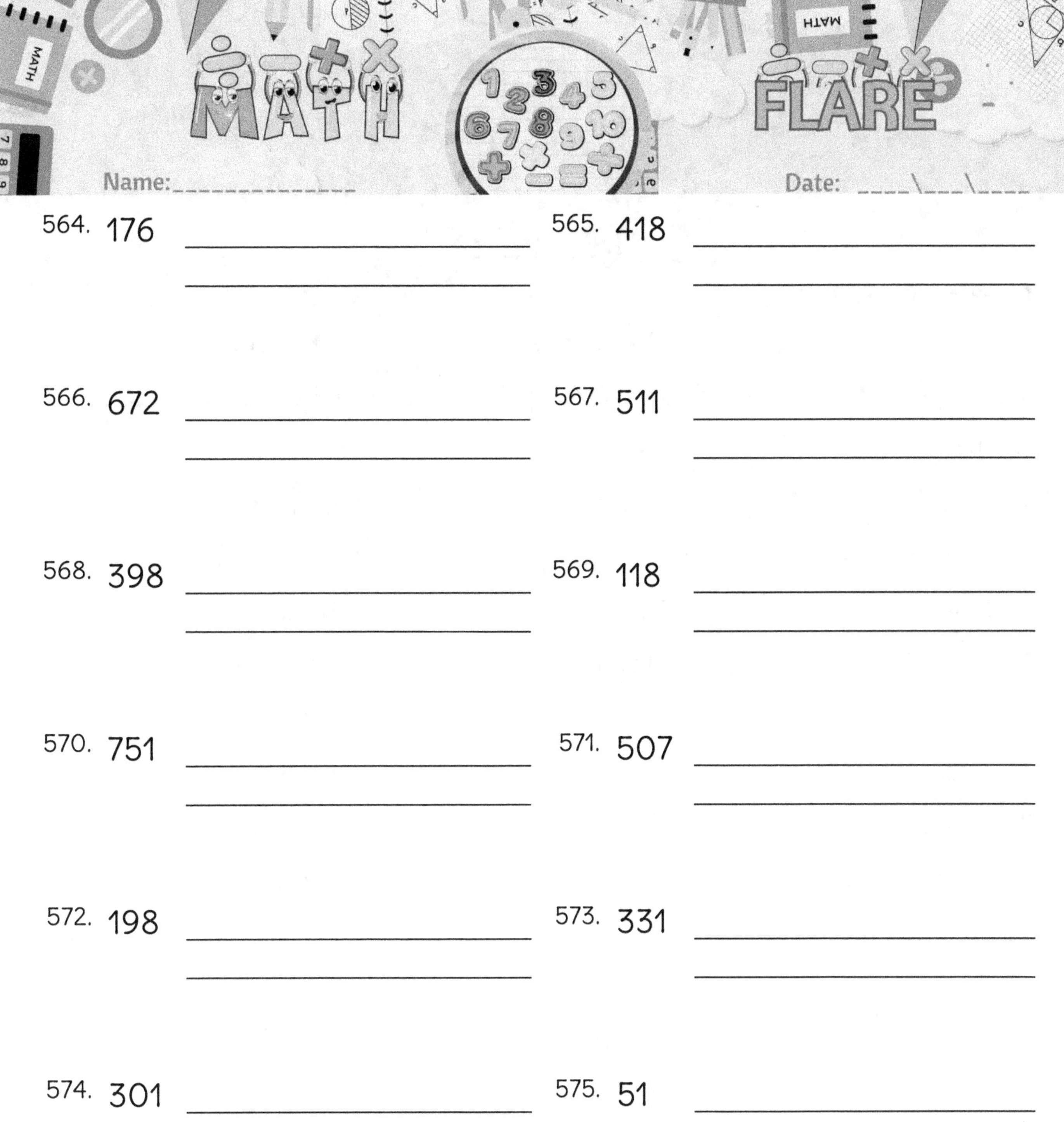

564. 176 _______________

565. 418 _______________

566. 672 _______________

567. 511 _______________

568. 398 _______________

569. 118 _______________

570. 751 _______________

571. 507 _______________

572. 198 _______________

573. 331 _______________

574. 301 _______________

575. 51 _______________

ANSWERS

Page 1: Place Value

1. 6 ones	2. 3 hundreds	3. 1 thousand
4. 2 thousands	5. 8 hundreds	6. 1 thousand
7. 7 thousands	8. 8 tens	9. 5 tens
10. 6 tens	11. 5 tens	12. 5 ones
13. 0 hundreds	14. 4 tens	15. 3 thousands
16. 8 tens	17. 7 ones	18. 5 thousands
19. 7 hundreds	20. 4 tens	21. 2 thousands
22. 4 thousands	23. 2 thousands	24. 8 thousands
25. 1 ten	26. 3 ones	27. 4 tens
28. 9 tens	29. 7 tens	30. 4 tens
31. 9 hundreds	32. 9 ones	33. 2 hundreds
34. 8 hundreds	35. 3 tens	36. 8 ones
37. 7 tens	38. 7 thousands	39. 7 hundreds
40. 5 tens	41. 8 hundreds	42. 5 ones
43. 2 tens	44. 6 hundreds	45. 6 thousands
46. 9 tens	47. 6 tens	48. 3 thousands
49. 4 thousands	50. 8 ones	51. 2 thousands
52. 9 thousands	53. 3 thousands	54. 0 ones
55. 2 tens	56. 6 thousands	57. 2 ones

58. 5 tens   59. 8 hundreds   60. 5 ones

61. 4 ones   62. 7 thousands   63. 6 ones

64. 1 ten   65. 8 thousands   66. 4 thousands

67. 7 thousands   68. 1 hundred   69. 3 hundreds

70. 8 tens   71. 3 hundreds   72. 7 tens

73. 5 tens   74. 9 tens   75. 8 thousands

76. 3 tens   77. 9 tens   78. 1 hundred

79. 9 tens   80. 4 thousands   81. 8 hundreds

82. 9 ones   83. 9 tens   84. 6 tens

85. 1 hundred   86. 4 ones   87. 9 ones

88. 0 ones   89. 2 tens   90. 6 tens

91. 2 hundreds   92. 8 hundreds

Page 7: Place Value: Expanded Notation

93. 9,443   94. 9,607   95. 4,812   96. 3,914   97. 7,630

98. 671   99. 6,477   100. 7,677   101. 9,252   102. 2,999

103. 474   104. 2,584   105. 563   106. 8,898   107. 7,814

108. 4,730   109. 7,914   110. 1,621   111. 7,269   112. 4,527

113. 3,461   114. 4,380   115. 4,416   116. 2,941   117. 5,710

118. 4,116   119. 4,163   120. 2,022   121. 202   122. 5,961

123. 5,268   124. 7,587   125. 2,216   126. 3,553   127. 6,107

128. 8,766   129. 6,760   130. 9,995   131. 7,811   132. 5,761

133. 2,004   134. 3,849   135. 9,630   136. 8,901   137. 409

138. 4,955   139. 6,371   140. 363   141. 2,321   142. 714

143. 392   144. 7,871   145. 4,399   146. 3,031   147. 6,084

148. 5,063   149. 5,192   150. 1,872   151. 8,202   152. 3,515

153. 6,507   154. 4,456   155. 7,476   156. 3,292   157. 7,730

158. 2,887   159. 370   160. 7,009   161. 2,793   162. 9,047

163. 7,969   164. 7,918   165. 3,808   166. 1,509   167. 2,524

168. 9,611   169. 4,750   170. 5,515   171. 2,534

Page 17:   Place Value: Expanded Notation

172. 9 thousands + 7 hundreds

173. 4 thousands + 1 hundred + 6 tens + 2 ones

174. 7 thousands + 8 hundreds + 7 tens + 6 ones

175. 8 thousands + 2 hundreds + 1 ten + 8 ones

176. 9 thousands + 7 hundreds + 3 tens + 6 ones

177. 9 thousands + 3 hundreds + 5 tens + 9 ones

178. 7 hundreds + 8 tens + 4 ones

179. 2 thousands + 1 hundred + 9 tens + 2 ones

180. 3 thousands + 1 ten + 2 ones

181. 6 thousands + 3 hundreds + 5 ones

182. 8 thousands + 7 hundreds + 1 ten

183. 9 thousands + 8 hundreds + 4 tens + 3 ones

184. 5 thousands + 6 hundreds + 3 tens + 8 ones

185. 7 thousands + 7 hundreds + 1 ten + 8 ones

186. 7 thousands + 7 hundreds + 1 ten + 4 ones

187. 5 thousands + 8 hundreds + 2 ones

188. 9 thousands + 6 hundreds + 6 tens + 6 ones

189. 8 thousands + 7 hundreds + 6 tens + 3 ones

190. 1 thousand + 8 hundreds + 7 tens + 3 ones

191. 7 thousands + 2 hundreds + 8 tens + 8 ones

192. 5 thousands + 6 hundreds + 6 ones

193. 2 thousands + 4 hundreds + 2 ones

194. 4 thousands + 9 hundreds + 4 tens + 8 ones

195. 2 thousands + 1 hundred + 8 tens

196. 5 thousands + 2 hundreds + 1 ten + 2 ones

197. 4 thousands + 7 hundreds + 3 tens + 7 ones

198. 9 thousands + 7 hundreds + 9 tens + 8 ones

199. 9 thousands + 3 hundreds + 8 tens + 5 ones

200. 6 thousands + 7 hundreds + 1 ten + 8 ones

201. 6 thousands + 7 hundreds + 3 tens + 5 ones

202. 4 thousands + 8 tens + 5 ones

203. 4 thousands + 5 hundreds + 5 tens + 9 ones

204. 2 thousands + 3 hundreds + 1 ten + 6 ones

205. 4 thousands + 5 ones

206. 4 thousands + 7 hundreds + 6 tens + 3 ones

207. 2 thousands + 9 hundreds + 7 tens + 9 ones

208. 6 thousands + 1 hundred + 1 ten + 5 ones

209. 5 thousands + 6 hundreds + 2 tens

210. 8 thousands + 6 hundreds + 8 tens + 6 ones

211. 1 thousand + 5 hundreds + 3 tens + 6 ones

212. 4 hundreds + 9 tens + 2 ones

213. 2 thousands + 6 hundreds + 1 ten + 2 ones

214. 3 thousands + 2 hundreds + 1 ten + 4 ones

215. 5 thousands + 8 hundreds + 2 tens + 8 ones

216. 5 thousands + 8 hundreds + 5 tens + 9 ones

217. 3 thousands + 7 hundreds + 2 tens + 5 ones

218. 9 thousands + 2 hundreds + 8 tens + 7 ones

219. 5 thousands + 6 hundreds + 2 tens + 9 ones

220. 6 hundreds + 6 tens + 4 ones

221. 6 thousands + 3 hundreds + 6 ones

222. 2 thousands + 1 hundred + 6 tens + 2 ones

223. 8 thousands + 3 hundreds + 7 tens + 4 ones

224. 6 thousands + 6 hundreds + 3 tens + 7 ones

225. 4 hundreds + 6 tens + 1 one

226. 7 thousands + 2 hundreds + 9 tens + 9 ones

227. 9 thousands + 2 hundreds + 1 ten + 4 ones

228. 5 thousands + 6 hundreds + 9 tens + 7 ones

229. 3 thousands + 6 ones

230. 5 thousands

231. 9 thousands + 5 hundreds + 6 tens

232. 1 thousand + 3 hundreds + 9 tens + 8 ones

233. 5 thousands + 4 hundreds + 7 tens + 3 ones

234. 6 thousands + 2 hundreds + 7 tens + 6 ones

235. 2 thousands + 2 hundreds + 2 tens + 2 ones

236. 4 thousands + 1 hundred + 5 tens + 2 ones

237. 7 thousands + 5 hundreds + 2 tens + 7 ones

238. 1 thousand + 6 hundreds + 3 tens + 5 ones

239. 2 thousands + 9 hundreds + 5 tens + 6 ones

Page 24: Place Value: Expanded Notation

240. 3,853	241. 2,258	242. 7,944	243. 7,608	244. 6,427
245. 3,325	246. 9,932	247. 9,277	248. 9,215	249. 5,138
250. 4,351	251. 7,200	252. 1,751	253. 6,423	254. 1,083
255. 2,292	256. 9,026	257. 4,138	258. 3,381	259. 7,853
260. 9,953	261. 6,465	262. 4,781	263. 6,816	264. 9,256
265. 1,309	266. 1,206	267. 8,524	268. 9,599	269. 2,076

270. 2,409   271. 8,009   272. 6,211   273. 464   274. 1,246

275. 8,676   276. 606   277. 8,306   278. 8,601   279. 2,269

280. 6,192   281. 2,234   282. 7,257   283. 3,988   284. 9,138

285. 429   286. 4,104   287. 7,571   288. 205   289. 4,883

290. 7,408   291. 2,192   292. 1,806   293. 8,190   294. 3,225

295. 7,387   296. 7,476   297. 1,130   298. 8,351   299. 5,119

300. 2,120   301. 1,410   302. 9,678   303. 7,140   304. 2,730

305. 6,341   306. 990   307. 1,288   308. 5,178   309. 2,407

310. 1,687   311. 720   312. 5,536   313. 1,113   314. 1,662

315. 7,720   316. 9,207   317. 794   318. 7,677   319. 8,828

320. 7,204   321. 3,633

Page 31: Place Value: Expanded Notation

322. 8,000 + 300 + 10 + 9   323. 4,000 + 700 + 10 + 6

324. 4,000 + 600 + 60 + 7   325. 200 + 10 + 8

326. 6,000 + 200 + 4   327. 8,000 + 20

328. 7,000 + 200 + 30 + 8   329. 3,000 + 800 + 50 + 8

330. 1,000 + 200 + 1   331. 9,000 + 400 + 70 + 5

332. 9,000 + 900 + 50 + 4   333. 3,000 + 400 + 80 + 3

334. 100 + 40 + 9   335. 4,000 + 700 + 80 + 4

336. 2,000 + 500 + 50 + 6   337. 100 + 10 + 8

338. 1,000 + 200 + 50 + 9   339. 2,000 + 700 + 90 + 7

340. 9,000 + 400 + 30 + 8

341. 2,000 + 800 + 10 + 7

342. 2,000 + 300 + 90 + 4

343. 7,000 + 700 + 90 + 8

344. 3,000 + 100 + 90 + 7

345. 6,000 + 600 + 80 + 8

346. 6,000 + 600 + 50 + 5

347. 600 + 90 + 4

348. 6,000 + 500 + 20 + 9

349. 5,000 + 500 + 4

350. 8,000 + 100 + 70 + 9

351. 6,000 + 600 + 80 + 3

352. 3,000 + 400 + 50 + 2

353. 9,000 + 500 + 20 + 2

354. 7,000 + 900 + 10 + 4

355. 8,000 + 400 + 80 + 6

356. 3,000 + 80 + 9

357. 4,000 + 900 + 60 + 2

358. 2,000 + 400 + 70 + 4

359. 2,000 + 500 + 10 + 3

360. 100 + 30 + 9

361. 2,000 + 900 + 60 + 9

362. 4,000 + 40 + 9

363. 1,000 + 300 + 20 + 1

364. 1,000 + 200 + 7

365. 2,000 + 200 + 10 + 1

366. 700 + 60 + 5

367. 2,000 + 50 + 4

368. 900 + 60 + 5

369. 6,000 + 800 + 70 + 7

370. 5,000 + 100 + 60 + 6

371. 9,000 + 90

372. 9,000 + 500 + 30 + 4

373. 4,000 + 800 + 80

374. 9,000 + 300 + 80 + 9

375. 4,000 + 300 + 80 + 7

376. 1,000 + 200 + 40

377. 500 + 20 + 2

378. 1,000 + 500 + 20

379. 7,000 + 900 + 70 + 8

380. 3,000 + 500 + 60 + 2

381. 5,000 + 500 + 10 + 1

382. 1,000 + 400 + 90 + 2

383. 1,000 + 700 + 30 + 5

384. 5,000 + 600 + 70 + 7

385. 4,000 + 500 + 10 + 7

386. 6,000 + 20 + 4

387. 400 + 30 + 3

388. 5,000 + 500 + 60 + 8

389. 1,000 + 600 + 60 + 2

390. 1,000 + 600 + 90 + 6

391. 7,000 + 500 + 90 + 3

392. 7,000 + 600 + 40 + 3

393. 8,000 + 700 + 40 + 5

394. 2,000 + 600 + 60

395. 6,000 + 400 + 70

396. 8,000 + 700 + 60 + 7

397. 1,000 + 70 + 4

398. 6,000 + 500 + 90 + 2

399. 900 + 80 + 8

400. 5,000 + 900 + 20 + 4

401. 4,000 + 600 + 2

402. 9,000 + 700 + 20 + 8

403. 9,000 + 600 + 50 + 1

Page 38:   Place Value: Expanded Notation

404. 340	405. 9,088	406. 7,148	407. 8,571	408. 134
409. 3,528	410. 7,247	411. 2,568	412. 3,443	413. 4,495
414. 8,950	415. 4,627	416. 1,478	417. 2,315	418. 5,643
419. 6,689	420. 6,186	421. 334	422. 6,485	423. 9,301
424. 5,183	425. 7,572	426. 1,448	427. 790	428. 2,221
429. 2,920	430. 5,619	431. 167	432. 3,929	433. 533
434. 2,055	435. 8,959	436. 5,782	437. 1,840	438. 1,396
439. 6,588	440. 7,368	441. 7,452	442. 299	443. 2,040
444. 4,415	445. 9,127	446. 4,151	447. 3,148	448. 9,795

449. 8,032   450. 4,994   451. 6,453   452. 5,430   453. 9,902

454. 4,801   455. 5,591   456. 8,116   457. 427   458. 4,469

459. 2,767   460. 7,641   461. 6,359   462. 6,350   463. 7,214

464. 7,908   465. 7,080   466. 8,638   467. 2,910   468. 2,441

469. 9,990   470. 8,843   471. 9,636   472. 920   473. 9,054

474. 9,320   475. 8,732   476. 36   477. 4,446   478. 4,888

479. 6,055   480. 3,422   481. 8,299

Page 48: Place Value: Expanded Notation

482. one hundred

483. four hundred nineteen

484. seven hundred ninety-two

485. nine hundred sixteen

486. four hundred seventy-four

487. four hundred three

488. five hundred seventy-three

489. six hundred forty-six

490. eighty-five

491. five hundred thirty-six

492. seven hundred thirty-seven

493. eight hundred sixty-two

494. eight hundred ninety-four

495. one hundred two

496. one hundred eleven

497. three hundred nine

498. four hundred thirteen

499. seven hundred thirty-three

500. fifty

501. one hundred twenty-five

502. seventy-two

503. nine hundred seventy-nine

504. nine hundred eighteen

505. five hundred fifty-three

506. six hundred thirty-seven

507. fifty-nine

508. six hundred seven

509. five hundred fifty-six

510. three hundred sixty-seven

511. five hundred fifty-four

512. eight hundred forty-one

513. nine hundred thirty-four

514. nine hundred thirty-three

515. two hundred seventeen

516. nine hundred twenty-eight

517. eight hundred seventy-four

518. two hundred thirty-five

519. four hundred sixty-one

520. seven hundred seventeen

521. five hundred ninety-eight

522. nine hundred fourteen

523. three hundred forty-nine

524. two hundred twenty-seven

525. two hundred thirty

526. twelve

527. eight hundred thirty

528. seven hundred sixty-three

529. six hundred ninety-five

530. thirty-two

531. seven hundred fifty-five

532. two hundred nineteen

533. seven hundred fifty-nine

534. one hundred twenty

535. five hundred

536. two hundred fifty-seven

537. three hundred sixty-three

538. eight hundred thirty-five

539. three hundred forty-five

540. nine hundred sixty-five

541. ninety-two

542. nine hundred eighty-one

543. eight hundred ninety-five

544. nine hundred sixty

545. five hundred sixty-four

546. eight hundred ninety-three

547. three hundred eighty

548. five hundred thirty-nine

549. four hundred ninety-nine

550. five hundred eighty-eight

551. four hundred six

552. four hundred seventy-three

553. sixty-six

554. five hundred seventy

555. three hundred twenty-five

556. six hundred twenty-six

557. two hundred twenty-eight

558. eight hundred forty-three

559. eight hundred sixty

560. three hundred thirty-six

561. seven hundred ninety-eight

562. two hundred eighty-five

563. seven hundred sixteen

564. one hundred seventy-six

565. four hundred eighteen

566. six hundred seventy-two

567. five hundred eleven

568. three hundred ninety-eight

569. one hundred eighteen

570. seven hundred fifty-one

571. five hundred seven

572. one hundred ninety-eight

573. three hundred thirty-one

574. three hundred one

575. fifty-one